TABLE OF CONTENTS

INTRODUCTION...1

CHAPTER 1: THE PERIOD OF U.S. RELIANCE ON THE DRAFT.................3

    The Spanish American War and the Phillipine Insurrection.....................4

    World War I...5

    World War II and Subsequent Reforms..9

    The Cold War..11

        Berlin (1961-1962)..13

        Cuba Missile Crisis (1962)...15

        McNamara Reforms..16

    Vietnam Era..19

        The Pueblo Crisis (1968)...21

        Tet Offensive 1968...25

        Total Force Policy (Post-Vietnam)..27

CHAPTER 2: NO DRAFT AND THE PERSIAN GULF WAR..........................29

    The Abrams Doctrine...29

    The Total Force Policy During Desert Shield and Desert Storm..............36

    More Mobilization Authority..55

    Reforms after the Persian Gulf War...56

CHAPTER 3: U.S. MILITARY AT WAR AFTER 9-11.................................61

    Engagement with American Society...65

CHAPTER 4: CONCLUSION...67

BIBLIOGRAPHY..71

INTRODUCTION

The United States is fighting a war in Afghanistan that has lasted longer than any war in its history. In this war, the United States military has relied heavily on the contributions of its reserve component because the active force is not large enough to handle the burden alone. The last time the draft provided augmentation to the active force was in 1973. Since then, the active force has become increasingly dependent upon the reserve components for augmentation. The evolution to a fully-integrated reserve component has been painful at times. From the Spanish-American War though the war in Vietnam, the United States relied partly on the draft to generate manpower for the forces that would go to war. After Vietnam, the U.S. adopted an all-volunteer force. The Total Force Policy relied on the reserve components to provide additional capability to the active forces for national emergencies. After the Persian Gulf War, the military had to make significant changes to laws and policies to ensure successful integration of the reserves for future conflicts, including the current war in Afghanistan.

In every conflict of U.S. history, the performance of the reserve forces was proportional to their level of training readiness. Those conflicts where the reserve components did not perform as well as expected indicated poor training preparation of the reserves. The reserve leadership was not properly trained; the reserve units were not equipped to train properly; or the reserves were not utilized in a manner for which they were trained. Following each conflict, the perceived performance of the reserve components brought about changes to law and policies to address future issues. Laws and policies evolved to provide the framework for total force integration that we utilize as a nation, today. This paper argues that the individual Services must systematically test the reserve components to ensure training readiness for the Total Force. Training readiness establishes the foundation for a solid relationship between the active and reserve forces of a Service thus ensuring our nation is prepared for future conflicts.

Chapter One traces the roots of current policies affecting the reserve components developed from the Spanish-American War through the ending of the draft and the war in Vietnam. Chapter Two reviews the post-draft era and describes the further evolution of policies and legislation affecting the reserve components through the Persian Gulf War. Chapter Three explains the importance of sustaining training readiness of the reserves both for the current conflicts and in the future. Chapter Four concludes with recommendations for all Services to facilitate maintaining training readiness in the reserve components for future conflicts.

CHAPTER 1: THE PERIOD OF U.S. RELIANCE ON THE DRAFT

For almost sixty years, from the First World War to the end of the war in Vietnam, when the United States went to war, the draft provided augmentation to the active military forces. The draft ended with the US withdrawal from Vietnam. Coincident to the end of the draft, the U.S. began to rely on an all-volunteer force. Secretary of Defense Laird announced the end of the draft for Vietnam, January 27, 1973. The beginning of a new Total Force Policy era began. From the Spanish-American War to the end of the draft, profound changes transformed American society and its military to create the conditions necessary for a successful all-volunteer force. This path did not follow a straight course, but twisted and turned throughout two world wars and much of the Cold War to arrive at the end of the draft. The changes in the U.S. military during this time included the creation of a reserve force that would be large enough and capable enough to respond to worldwide contingencies.

The first turn along this path to the all-volunteer force was the Militia Act of 1903 which created the dual-status National Guard from the colonial militias. The National Guard would serve both state governors and also the President in times of national emergency. A natural tension developed between the citizen soldiers of the reserve component and professional soldiers of the active component Army prior to the First World War that fostered an impetus for later change. In other instances, the performance or lack of performance of the reserve components during World War II invited change.

Another important turn was the National Security Act of 1947, which created the Air Force, the Air Force Reserve and the Air National Guard. The Armed Forces Reserve

Act of 1952 followed, by establishing the Ready Reserve, the Standby Reserve and the Retired Reserve. The Ready Reserve, which included the entire National Guard had an authorized strength of 1.5 million and could be mobilized by the president for national emergencies. The Standby and Retired Reserve provided further protection from all but full manpower mobilization for World War II veterans and the retired military. During the Spanish-American War members of the state militias fought well alongside their federal counterparts.[1] However, during World War II, National Guard Divisions did not perform measurably better than divisions formed from conscripts. This chapter will sequentially examine seventy-five years of conflicts and the resulting changes to law intended to improve integration and readiness of the reserve forces. This evolution of the Armed Forces made the all-volunteer force possible.

The Spanish-American War and the Philippine Insurrection

The Spanish-American War marked the first time in American history the country needed an expeditionary Army. The state militias' participation in the Spanish-American War and the Philippine Insurrection earned high regard for the citizen-soldiers with the American people. In 1898, the Army had a force of 28,000 men, not nearly enough to invade Cuba, Puerto Rico or to quell the Philippine Insurrection. President William McKinley relied upon the state governors to raise volunteer regiments that contributed over 180,000 men to the war effort. Militia volunteers made up the majority of forces sent to the Philippines and Puerto Rico by a factor of five to one. One of the more famous units was the 1st U.S. Volunteer Cavalry, consisting of militia units from Arizona

---

[1] Michael D. Doubler, *I Am the Guard: A History of the National Guard, 1636-2000* (Washington, DC: Army National Guard, 2001), 135.

and New Mexico, better known as the "Rough Riders."[2] Without the militia volunteers, the Army would not have had expeditionary capacity and might not have been capable of putting down the Phillipine Insurrection.

Following the Spanish-American War, Secretary of War, Elihu Root, wanted to dramatically increase the size of the Army, in the event of a possible war with one of the major powers in Europe. Congress believed that increasing the size of the active Army would prove too expensive and too contrary with American political tradition. Secretary Root proposed using the militias to bolster the active Army. The Militia Act of 1903 repealed the Militia Act of 1792 and converted the state militias to the National Guard. This created a dual-status force with obligations to both the federal and state governments. In exchange for federal funding, the National Guard had to conform to standard organization and training within five years. The new guardsmen were to attend mandatory training, twenty-four drill periods per year and five days of summer training each year. For the first time, former militia members would receive pay for the five days of summer training, (although not for the weekend sessions). The National Guard would also have federally provided arms and equipment to train with.[3]

World War I

In response to the war in Europe, that was raging during the early twentieth century, the Preparedness Movement in the United States fostered the political will for increasing the size of the Army. The War Department desired an Army large enough for expeditionary operations, without having to rely on augmentation from the National

---

[2] Ibid., 129.
[3] Ibid., 140-144.

Guard. The War Department proposed in its Continental Army Plan, drafting 500,000 men to bolster the ranks of the active Army in lieu of calling up the National Guard. The National Guard would be used for domestic defense such as manning coastal artillery stations and protecting key strategic sites. The expense of drafting so many, without using the National Guard, did not set well with several congressional leaders who were able to convince President Wilson to withdraw his support for the Continental Army Plan.

Congress responded to the need for a larger Army by passing the The National Defense Act of 1916 which created a force of Army Regulars, Reservists and Guardsmen. The Act provided funding for 48 drill periods and 15 days of annual training that continues today. Congress increased funding to the states for training in exchange for greater federal control over the National Guard. Greater federal control addressed the reliability and legality concerns of employing the National Guard in overseas combat. Durning national emergencies Guardsmen would be drafted into the Army as individuals and then serve as part of their state units in the Regular Army. The National Guard would now be the nation's primary trained reserve.[4] These reforms allowed for better integration of the National Guard with the active force when the U.S. entered what would become World War I in 1917.

At the time the United States entered the war in Europe, it needed to quickly raise an Army. President Wilson saw the draft as part of the solution that would least impact the American economy, especially the industrial and agricultural production. He directed the War Department to draft legislation that would correct the defects of the Civil War draft.

---

[4] Ibid., 156-159.

The Selective Service Act of 1917 prohibited enlistment bounties and allowed deferments in the case of critical jobs for industry or agriculture.[5]

Major Douglas MacArthur, who was in charge of the War Department's Bureau of Information convinced the Secretary of the War, Newton Baker, and President Wilson to fully employ Guard units arguing that voluntary enlistments would bring Guard units up to full strength and those units could be effectively trained for combat. MacArthur would later comment that he steadfastly shared his father's belief in the citizen-soldier.[6] In July of 1917, President Wilson called the National Guard to active duty. Using the authorities from the National Defense Act of 1916 and the Selective Service Act of 1917, the federal government mobilized the National Guard as individuals, instead of units, into the Army to preclude any confusion about fealty to the states over the federal government. At the direction of General Pershing, the Allied Expeditionary Force (AEF) was an integrated force of Regulars, Guardsmen, Reservists and Draftees. General Pershing concluded that the Army's divisional structure was inadequate for sustained trench warfare. He reorganized the Army, into "square divisions" that consisted of infantry, artillery, engineer, signal, supply and medical units. The sixteen Guard divisions that reported for training were completely reorganized and renumbered in accordance with the AEF numbering system. Regular Army divisions were numbered, 1-25 so Guard divisions were renumbered 26-75. Some of the Guard units traced their original numerical designations back to the colonial militia, so the renumbering of units angered many Guardsmen. The states had more units than the square divisions required which resulted

---

[5] Ibid., 168-169.

[6] Stephen M. Duncan, Citizen Warriors: America's National Guard and Reserve Forces & the Politics of National Security (Novato, CA: Presidio, 1997), 57.

7

in excess Guard units. Major MacArthur recommended forming a "Rainbow Division" from these excess units of 26 states. To preclude any one state from claiming its Guard units were the first to deploy, the Rainbow Division would be the first Guard division to deploy to France. Secretary of War Baker approved the idea and promoted MacArthur to Lieutenant Colonel to enable him to serve as the new division's chief of staff. Major General William A. Mann, a Regular Army officer, became the division commander.[7]

The assignment of a Regular Army officer to command the Rainbow Division infuriated several Guard generals who considered themselves better candidates. The Army readily assigned Regular officers to Guard units whenever the Guard officers were physically unfit, lacking requisite leadership skills, or professional knowledge. This solved the immediate problem of finding competent leaders for the Guard units but did nothing to improve professional leadership development in the National Guard. The caliber of National Guard leadership had declined under the federally funded and equipped forces from the purely voluntary, personally equipped militias that fought in the Spanish-American War. Part of this was a result of the rapid expansion in the size of the Guard from the state militias without sufficient time to develop a new generation of leaders. Another factor was the Army's failure to address the leadership problem during the interwar years. The leadership replacement policy caused friction at the training camps and created an inhospitable hierarchy: Regulars disdained the Guardsmen while the Guardsmen despised the draftees.[8]

---

[7] Doubler, 167-174.

[8] Ibid., 175.

World War II and Subsequent Reforms

The Guard leadership problem followed the Army into World War II. General Omar Bradley described the state of leadership in the eighteen National Guard divisions mobilized for World War II:

> Almost without exception, the senior commanders – the generals and the colonels – were political appointees who were militarily incompetent. A high percentage of the junior officers were over-age and physically unfit. (In June 1941, a study found the 22 percent of all Guard first lieutenants were over forty)....McNair, who was responsible for training the Guard divisions, had to fire almost every officer in the Guard from major general through colonel, and a large percentage of the lower-ranking officers.[9]

The issue of leadership directly impacted readiness and plagued Guard units throughout World War II. Prior to his death at Normandy, LTG Lesley J. McNair wrote a scathing memorandum to General Marshall in the spring of 1944 expressing his opinion that the Guard had, "contributed nothing to National Defense," that its history since mobilization, "was one of unsatisfactory training, physical condition, discipline, morale and particularly leadership." He further recommended, "the National Guard be dispensed with as a component of the Army of the United States."[10]

Using the lessons learned in World War II, Congress began a series of reforms to expand the Services, give the president greater access to the reserves and to reform the National Guard. Congressional reforms focused on organization of the armed forces and did not address the issues of training, physical condition, discipline, morale and leadership that had degraded readiness in the National Guard during the war.

---

[9] Omar Nelson Bradley and Clay Blair, *A General's Life: An Autobiography*, (New York: Simon and Schuster,1983), 108.

[10] Ibid., 208.

The National Security Act of 1947 was the first of these organizational reforms. It established a separate Department of the Air Force, to include the Air Force Reserve and Air National Guard. [11] The law also tasked the National Guard Bureau with duties similarly tasked to it for the Department of the Army, making it the channel of communication between the Department of the Air Force and the several states in all matters pertaining to the Air National Guard. [12]

The next reform gave Congress and the president greater control over the reserves. The Selective Service Act of 1948, enacted in June of that year, gave Congress or the president the authority to call-up the Reserve components at their discretion for reasons of national security in excess of the Regular components as are necessary for a balanced force, so long as the necessity exists. [13]

Named after its chairman, the Assistant Secretary of the Army, Gordon Gray, the Gray Board was the first official post-World War II study reviewing the status of reserve forces. [14] The Gray Board found that the National Guard, with its dual state and federal allegiances, was not suitable for the Cold War. Additionally, the board criticized reserve forces for having experience but lacking in readiness. The Gray Board recommended the merger of the National Guard and the Reserves into a federally controlled force called the National Guard of the United States. [15] Although Secretary of Defense Forrestal

---

[11] Public Law No. 80-253, *National Security Act of 1947*, 61 Stat 495, 502, July 26, 1947, http://research.archives.gov/description/299856 (accessed January 15, 2012).

[12] 61 Stat 495, 503, http://research.archives.gov/description/299856 (accessed January 15, 2012).

[13] Public Law No. 80-759, *Selective Service Act of 1948*, 62 Stat 604, June 24, 1948, http://www.ssa.gov/OP_Home/comp2/F080-759.html (accessed January 15, 2012).

[14] I.M. McQuiston, "History of the Reserves Since the Second World War," *Military Affairs*, (no. 1, 1953), 23-24.

[15] Doubler, 229.

convened the board, he did not endorse its final recommendations presented in 1948.[16]

Congress lacked the political will for a controversial reform mostly aimed at efficiencies.

The National Guard and the National Guard Association of the United States had

effectively lobbied Congress, not to merge the reserve components.[17]

The Cold War

The Selective Service Act of 1948 gave Congress the additional authority over the

reserves that it wanted without the political controversy associated with the Gray Board

recommendation. The Act addressed authorities for the president and Congress to call-up

the reserves. However, during the partial mobilization for the Korean War, the real issue

again, became the readiness of the reserve component forces.[18] The Korean War saw the

largest call-up in the post-World War II era, with 806,000 reservists mobilized from a

force of 2.5 million (32 percent activation rate). There were no authorites for the Army

to activate drilling reservists as individual replacements. This forced the Army to

mobilize entire units when what it needed were mostly individual replacements. This led

to entire reserve units sitting at home while non-drilling reservists were called up. Non-

drilling veterans from World War II went ahead of drilling non-veterans. Reservists who

were fathers, skilled techicians and students were called up while draftees with the same

situation were excused. There was an exemption from the draft for members of the

---

[16] National Defense Research Institute (U.S.), *Assessing the Structure and Mix of Future Active and Reserve Forces: Final Report to the Secretary of Defense* (Santa Monica, CA: RAND, 1992), 26-27.

[17] Doubler, 229.

[18] Abbott A. Brayton, "American Reserve Policies Since World War II," *Military Affairs* (no. 4, 1972), 140.

National Guard for young men between the ages of 17 and 18-1/2. A draft eligible male between those ages could join the National Guard and become exempt from the draft.[19]

The Armed Forces Reserve Act of 1952 attempted to correct the inequities of the partial mobilization for the Korean War. The act established the policy that the reserve components would be maintained to provide both trained units and qualified individuals to be available for active duty in the Armed Forces of the United States in time of war or national emergency.[20] The act also established the seven reserve components: the National Guard of the United States, the Army Reserve, the Naval Reserve, The Marine Corps Reserve, the Air Force Reserve, the Air National Guard of the United States, and the Coast Guard Reserve. Additionally, the Act created three levels of reserves (ready, standby and retired), while setting the authorized troop strength of 1.5 million for the Ready Reserve.[21] Individual Reservists and Guardsmen could volunteer for active duty, which would allow them to avoid mobilization.[22]

Following the Reserve Forces Act of 1952, Congress passed the Reserve Forces Act of 1955, which raised the ceiling to 2.9 million persons. The Act also gave the president authority to call up to 1 million Ready Reservists to duty, in case of national emergency.[23]

---

[19] James L. Lacy, "Naval Reserve Forces: The Historical Experience with Involuntary Recalls," (Alexandria, VA: Center for Naval Analysis, 1986), 6.

[20] Public Law No. 66-476, *Armed Forces Reserve Act of 1952*, 66 Stat 481,482, July 1, 1952.

[21] 66 Stat 483.

[22] Charles J. Gross, "A Chronological History of the Air National Guard and its Antecedents, 1908-2007," April 2, 2007, http://www.ngb.army.mil/features/AF60th/ANG-CHRON_1908_2007.doc (accessed January 15, 2012).

[23] Public Law No. 84-305, 69 Stat 598, 599, August 9, 1955.

President Eisenhower, strongly influenced by his own observations during World War II, questioned the value of reserves as a military force. Congress responded by mandating a minimum force level of 700,000 troops, creating such a large force that would ensure the relevance of the Ready Reserve.[24] The minimum force level did little to convince Eisenhower of the value of the reserve component. His principal complaint, voiced during his last year in office, was the excessive size of the reserve components. At a cost of $80 million a year, the reserve force had no military value and was not a serious factor in military planning.[25]

Berlin (1961-1962)

The Berlin Crisis provided the first opportunity to utilize the authority granted a president by the Reserve Forces Act of 1955 to mobilize up to 1 million Ready Reservists in the case of national emergency. The Berlin Crisis taught the United States that a massive mobilization takes much longer than expected and is not without unforeseen consequences.

In April of 1961, newly elected President Kennedy authorized the CIA-backed Bay of Pigs invasion. The failure of that invasion signaled to the Soviets that the new president might have an Achilles' heel.[26] In June of 1961, at the Vienna summit, Soviet Premier Khrushchev repeated previous demands to "solve the occupation status of West Berlin, making it a free city," and to limit access to West Berlin solely at the sufferance of the

---

[24] U.S. Army Center for Military History, Office of the Chief of Military History, " Chapter 26: The Army and the New Look," *American Military History*, April 27, 2001, 591, http://www.history.army.mil/books/AMH/AMH-26.htm (accessed May 23, 2012).

[25] Lacy, 7.

[26] Brian Faltinson, "A Crisis Hits Home," *National Guard*, August 2011, 93.

East German state. [27] Khrushchev indicated to Kennedy that by year's end, the Soviet Union would sign a separate treaty with East Germany, barring American, British and French access to Berlin. Kennedy responded by stating that the United States would risk war to protect access to Berlin. He called for an increase of $3.25 billion to the defense budget to increase the size of the military and to for support mobilization of the reserves. [28] On August 1, 1961, Congress passed SJ Res 120 authorizing the president to call up any reserve unit, or reserve member not assigned to a unit, for not more than 12 consecutive months. Congress limited the involuntary mobilization to 250,000 Ready Reservists. The Kennedy administration sought to increase the size of the active force by 300,000. This was to be accomplished in priority, by voluntary enlistments, increased draft calls, involuntary extensions to active duty, and lastly, recall of reservists. The combined active force of the three departments increased in strength by 328,000 of which 148,000 were recalled reservists. [29] The Army planned to mobilize enough reservists stateside, to allow six active divisions to deploy to Germany. [30]

It took four months to complete the call-up of all three Services. The last reserve unit mobilized was crew of a Navy destroyer reporting for duty on December 18, 1961 [31] By the time the destroyer crew reported for duty, the Berlin crisis was long over. [32] The Soviets began building the wall on August 13, 1961. The construction of the Berlin wall

---

[27] Lacy, 7.

[28] Faltinson, 93.

[29] Lacy, 7.

[30] Faltinson, 93.

[31] Lacy, 9.

[32] The involuntary mobilization for the Berlin Crisis had a widespread impact on American society. It even snared professional football players. The Green Bay Packers had three members mobilized from the Army Reserve: halfback Paul Hornung, linebacker Ray Nitschke and flanker Boyd Dowler, Faltinson, 95.

solved one of Khrushchev's immediate problems, which was the mass exodus of East Germans to the West. The wall solved Kennedy's problem of access to Berlin by solving Khrushchev's lesser problem of containment of East German refugees. [33] Despite the new presidential authorities allowing for involuntary mobilization of the reserves, the difficulties in rapidly mobilizing reserve forces, remained.

Cuba Missile Crisis (1962)

The Cuba Missile Crisis is more significant to the reserve forces not for their contributions, but for what became a lack of contributions due to the missteps of the Berlin Crisis. Secretary McNamara testified before Congress in support of HJ Res 876 and SJ Res 224, which essentially gave the President the same powers to call-up the reserves that he had with the Berlin Crisis. The President could order to active duty any unit or member of the Ready Reserve for not more than 12 consecutive months. However, not more than 150,000 members of the Ready Reserve could be on active duty, other than for training, without their consent. This was 100,000 less than had been authorized for the Berlin Crisis but roughly equal to the actual number of Ready Reservists recalled for Berlin.

The Cuba Missile Crisis relied primarily on the Navy to enforce the quarantine of Cuba, but the Navy had just released 8,343 reservists from the Berlin call-up. The Navy chose not to recall any reservists. [34]

---

[33] Lacy, 10.

[34] Ibid., 11.

McNamara Reforms

Not pleased with the call-up for the Berlin Crisis, Secretary of Defense Robert

McNamara believed he could restructure the reserve components to be more efficient at

lower cost to the taxpayer. McNamara proposed eliminating 717 units (58,000

personnel) from an original force of 8,734 units (700,000 personnel). Of the 29 divisions

remaining after the restructuring, six divisions would be high priority (ready to deploy in

eight weeks), two divisions would be conventional priority (ready to deploy in 12 weeks)

and 21 would be low priority (ready to deploy in 20-34 weeks). The six high priority

divisions would include 462,000 forces while the conventional priority and low priority

units would include 180,000. (The number of divisions is not representative of the

numbers of personnel involved). In essence, this restructuring would have reduced the

Ready Reserve from 700,000 to 462,000.[35]

In April of 1962, a subcommittee of the House Armed Services Committee reviewed

both McNamara proposals and conducted a "comprehensive inquiry into the defense

posture of the Reserve components of our Armed Forces."[36] The subcommittee report

was critical of both the Department of Defense testimony and the Army planners that

were more interested in remaining within budgetary guidelines than with the requirement

for increased readiness. Congress viewed McNamara's proposal as simply a realignment

of numbers without addressing either the difficulties the Reserves were having with

recruiting and retaining experienced senior enlisted personnel or addressing the

---

[35] Alice R. Buchalter and Seth Elan. *Historical Attempts to Reorganize the Reserve Components* (Washington DC: Library of Congress, 2007), 6.

[36] U.S. Congress, House of Representatives, Committee on Armed Services, Subcommittee No. 3, Military Reserve Posture Hearings, 87th Congress, 2d Session, April 16th, 1962, 5400.

equipment issues. In response to the rather strong rebuff from Congress, Secretary

McNamara scrapped his original proposal and restructured eight low readiness divisions

into eight high-priority brigades.[37]

In 1964, citing the need to increase readiness; eliminate all units for which there was

no military requirement; and to achieve cost savings, Secretary McNamara proposed

merging all Army reserve components under the National Guard. This was the opposite

of the Gray Board recommendation of 1948 to merge the National Guard with the Army

Reserves. McNamara issued a press release on December 12, 1964 for the proposed

realignment:

> 1) The force structure would consist exclusively of units for which there is a military requirement, including combat and combat support units together with base mobilization base units such as training divisions, garrison detachments and reception station augmentation detachments and would require a paid drill strength estimated at 550,000 men.
> 2) Five independent brigades would be added to the 11 currently in the structure, making a total of 16 independent brigades, which could be deployed as such or in association with other forces in the structure.
> 3) The entire force would be included in the structure for which the army purchases equipment; as a result equipment would be authorized for two additional divisions and five additional brigades.
> 4) The unit structure of the Guard and Reserve would be merged under the management of the National Guard.[38]

At the press conference, McNamara explained his reasoning: The total authorized

strength for the National Guard was 400,000; the total authorized strength for the Reserve

was 300,000. In both the Guard and Reserve, there were units for which there was a clear

military requirement and other units for which there was no military requirement. The

---

[37] Buchalter and Elan, 8.

[38] U.S.Congress, House of Representatives, Committee on Armed Services, Subcommittee Number 2, Merger of the Army Reserve Components, 89th Congress, 1st Session, March 25, 1965, 3557-3559.

total strength of forces required to support the war plans was 498,000. There were 21 divisions, 15 in the Guard and 6 in the Reserve, which were not needed for any war plans. Those 21 divisions amounted to 168,000 men in units that were not manned at levels needed for deployment and for which no equipment was being purchased. Furthermore, it would take less time to organize 21 new divisions, recruit and train new personnel than it would to distribute equipment to the present 21 divisions. The men in the 21 divisions not needed for the war plans were being wasted and the funds expended to support them were also being wasted. This new unit structure, that Secretary of Defense McNamara was proposing, would result in increased combat readiness, streamlined management and save $150 million annually.[39]

During the question and answer portion, McNamara clarified that the Army Reserve would continue to exist, but as individuals, not as units. Individuals in the Army Reserve would participate in summer training and could be called up in a national emergency. Additionally, there would be cost savings from eliminating the duplicate administrative structure.[40]

Many congressional representatives were incensed at McNamara for announcing a proposed major shift in policy at a press conference, rather than consulting with Congress first. A subcommittee of the House Armed Services Committee called McNamara to testify. The subcommittee chairman accused McNamara of violating the laws that established the reserve forces and Congress's responsibility for maintaining militias.[41]

---

[39] *Merger of the Army Reserve Components*, March 25, 1965, 3576.

[40] Ibid., 3577.

[41] Ibid., 3572.

The Reserve Officers Association lobbied Congress hard to reject McNamara's proposal to eliminate the Army Reserve.[42] This lobbying, combined with the residual ire evoked by McNamara's press conference, made it difficult for the subcommittee to look favorably on the proposal. In August of 1965, the subcommittee announced that based on extensive testimony that began on March 15, Secretary McNamara's proposal to merge the Army Reserve components would result in an immediate loss of combat readiness and was therefore not in the best interest of the nation.[43] Although citing McNamara's proposal as a threat to readiness, the Reserve Officers Association was protecting Army Reserve force structure. Its political strength easily overpowered the secretary of defense.

The Vietnam Era

During the same time that Secretary McNamara was sparring with the subcommittee of the House Armed Services Committee, he was at odds with President Johnson over calling up members of the Reserve and National Guard for service in Vietnam. McNamara recommended calling up 235,000 members of the reserve components, but Johnson, who believed such action would be too unpopular with the American people, rejected the idea. McNamara did create a 150,000-man force from the Guard and Reserve that trained intensively for service in Vietnam. However, that force never saw duty in Vietnam.

President Johnson's decision not to use the Reserve forces in Vietnam placed a terrible burden on the Army and likely made the war in Vietnam less popular with the American

---

[42] Brayton, 141.

[43] "Subcommittee Number 2 News Release of August 12, 1965, " *Merger of the Army Reserve Components*, 4454.

public. Johnson's decision had second order effects by forcing the Active Army to bolster its ranks with conscripts without access to the Reserve forces that were on every contingency plan. Committed Reservists saw their units deteriorate with an influx of those seeking to avoid the draft.[44] During the war in Vietnam, the Army National Guard only deployed to maintain civil order during race riots and antiwar protests, including the Watts section of Los Angeles in 1965.[45]

In September of 1965, Congress made its opposition to McNamara's proposal official with Public Law Number 89-213, the fiscal year (FY) 1966 Department of Defense appropriations. Congress would now appropriate funds for the Guard and Reserves as separate components.[46] Included in the law was a provision in Section 639 that prohibited the Secretary of Defense from transferring funds to realign or reorganize the Army Reserve Components, without the approval of Congress.[47] Congress further stipulated a new authorized strength of 380,000 for the Guard and 270,000 for the Army Reserves. This was less than the previous 400,000 and 300,000 respective authorizations; yet, it was far greater than the combined 498,000 authorizations that McNamara had proposed.

Not to have his reform efforts completely stymied by Congress, in 1967 McNamara assigned the Army Guard the role of combat and combat support while assigning the Army Reserves the role of combat service support.[48] Congress responded by passing the

---

[44] Lewis Sorley, "Reserve Components: Looking Back to Look Ahead," *Joint Force Quarterly*, no. 36 (2005): 19-20.

[45] Doubler, 263.

[46] Public Law 89-213, 79 Stat 863, 864, September 29, 1965.

[47] Public Law 89-213, 79 Stat 879-880.

[48] Doubler, 255-256.

Reserve Forces Bill of Rights and Vitalization Act.[49] This created the Selected Reserve

within the Ready Reserve for each of the Reserve components. The Ready Reserve was

now comprised of units forming the Selected Reserve and individuals not assigned to

units, forming the Individual Ready Reserve.[50] (There was no change to the remaining

two levels of the Standby Reserve and Retired Reserve). The Ready Reserve was now

comprised of units of the Selected Reserve and the Individual Ready Reserve for the

Reserve components of each Service. The House of Representatives advocated

establishing an authorized strength for the Selected Reserve, but the Senate did not agree.

The two branches of Congress resolved this by the provision that personnel

authorizations for the Selected Reserves shall be designated each year, by law, as a

condition for the appropriation of funds for pay and allowances for the reserve

components.[51]

Public Law Number 90-168 also created the position of Chief of Army Reserve

(CAR). The law specified that the CAR must be, as a minimum, a brigadier general who

has at least ten years commissioned service in the Army Reserve. The CAR would be

appointed by the president, confirmed by the Senate, and serve as the advisor to the Chief

of Staff of the Army on matters concerning matters of the Army Reserve.[52]

The Pueblo Crisis (1968)

On January 23, 1968, the North Korean Navy seized the intelligence ship, USS

Pueblo. Two days later, citing a need to strengthen the U.S. position in Korea, without

---

[49] Public Law Number 90-168, 81 Stat 521, December 1, 1967.

[50] Public Law Number 90-168, 81 Stat 521, 522.

[51] H.R. Rep. No. 90-925 (1967).

[52] Public Law Number 90-168, 81 Stat 521-523.

diverting resources from Southeast Asia, President Johnson ordered a partial mobilization.[53] Johnson invoked the authorities of the Department of Defense Authorization Bill of 1967 (PL89-687):

> Notwithstanding any other provision of the law, until June 30, 1968, the President may when he deems it necessary, to order to active duty any unit of the Ready Reserve of an armed force for the period of not to exceed twenty-four months.

The interpretation of "unit" was restricted to those units that trained and were organized for mobilization on active duty as units.[54] (This interpretation came from the definition of the Selected Reserve designated by the Reserve Forces Bill of Rights and Vitalization Act, PL 90-168, passed in December of 1967).

The Navy completed the call-up for the Pueblo Crisis on 24-hour notice. Three fighter and three attack Naval Reserve Air Squadrons reported for duty on January 26, 1968.[55] It is not clear why the Navy selected these six particular units and what the intended purpose of the mobilization was. A September 1968 Defense Department News release stated that the mobilization was to improve Navy aviation strength and to meet contingencies that might have occurred. An unsigned, undated Navy memorandum later explained that there was a short period of time while the reserve squadrons were undergoing refresher training that "policy decisions concerning their use were held in abeyance until a careful evaluation of various courses of action could be completed." The contingencies that these squadrons could have served against was very limited because they were equipped with aircraft needing modification for carrier use, 36 A-4s

---

[53] National Defense Research Institute Study, "Assessing the Structure and Mix of Future Active and Reserve Forces," 32.

[54] Lacy, 12.

[55] VF 661 (Washington, DC); VF 703 (Dallas, TX); VF 931 (Willow Grove, PA); VA 776 (Los Alamitos, CA); VA 831 (New York, NY); VA 873 Alameda, CA. (Lacy, 13).

and 36 F-8s. A later memorandum from the Office of the Secretary of Defense (OSD) attempted to explain the reason for selecting these particular squadrons: "…unit selections were hurried and based on readiness factors." This clarification contradicted the facts because these recalled squadrons had only 593 personnel assigned against 1,115 authorizations, or a personnel readiness of 53 percent.[56]

The Navy announced on September 17, 1968 that it would release all 593 naval air reservists before November 1. This announcement followed the announcement the previous week that the Navy would begin releasing 30,000 enlisted volunteers to save $48-million during the current fiscal year. The volunteers had enlisted under the "two by six" program, which required two years active duty followed by four years in the reserve. The projected savings would be part of the Navy's portion of the $3-billion in defense cuts, apart from Vietnam, that the President ordered. Representative Richard S. Schweiker, (R-PA), of the House Armed Services Committee assailed the Navy's action as a "disgraceful and outrageous injustice," for retaining the reservists on active duty when at the same time planning to release enlisted volunteers to save money. Previously, Representative Schweiker had referred to President Johnson's call-up of the reservists, two days after the Pueblo incident as an "outrageous sham." Mr. Schweiker explained that squadron VF-931 had been called up within 48 hours of the Pueblo incident and then waited four months with neither practice aircraft nor operational aircraft before deploying to Cecil Field, near Jacksonville, Florida. The men were then to become routine replacements in the Mediterranean, far removed from where the Pueblo was seized.

---

[56] Lacy, 13.

According to one of his aides, it was only after Representative Schweiker's statements became public that the Pentagon agreed to release the reservists.[57]

The Navy mobilization for the Pueblo incident highlighted numerous problems that the Services were struggling with regarding partial mobilization. The Naval Air Reserve was not well suited to a partial mobilization. Each aircraft had four separate aircrews. This made it extremely cost effective for training, but not efficient for partial mobilization. The Navy selected the squadrons based on readiness factors; those factors only included percentages of equipment and personnel, not the requirements for their active duty assignments. The six mobilized squadrons were carrier units, but their aircraft were not combat ready. The F-8As could not operate from carriers without gear modifications. The F-8As also had manual fire control systems, which limited their operations to daylight and clear skies. The A-4Bs had no Shrike (anti-radar) or Walleye (television controlled) missile capability, and no armor plating. The radar on the A-4B was not advanced enough for contour flying. Because the Navy only mobilized six squadrons instead of following the Navy's Logistic Support Plan, the squadrons lacked requisite personnel from maintenance and weapons training units. There was no authority to mobilize the additional 522 personnel required, to bring the squadrons up to their full authorization of 1,115. The Navy augmented the reserve squadrons by bringing in 206 volunteers, 229 Training and Administration of the Reserve (TAR) – now called Full-Time Support (FTS) service members, and 107 personnel cross-leveled from its active force. Housing availability for the reservists was also a problem. The mobilized reservists lodged in off-base hotels, two to a room, for the initial few months, until on

---

[57] Benjamin Welles, "Navy to Release 593 Air Reserves," *New York Times*, September 17, 1968.

base facilities became available. The pilot qualifications were not current with carrier landings or with dropping live ordnance .[58] The many difficulties in getting just six, half-strength squadrons, soured the Navy on the difficulties with partial mobilization.

Tet Offensive 1968

President Johnson faced increasing political pressure against his earlier decision not to call-up the Guard and Reserves for Vietnam. It became increasingly unpopular for paid drilling reservists to be draft-exempt while increasing numbers of young men were being drafted from civilian life. The quality of the reserve forces declined. Dedicated reservists became discouraged over not being able to participate in the nation's war while the ranks of the reserves gained a greater number of young men just trying to avoid the draft.[59] Furthermore, the Reserves were viewed with increasing disdain by the Active forces as a haven for draft deserters. On January 30, 1968, the Vietnamese holiday of Tet, North Vietnamese forces launched an attack with approximately 80,000 regular and irregular forces. The American Public was shocked. Americans had believed prior to the offensive that the Communist forces were incapable of launching a large-scale attack.. U.S. and South Vietnamese forces quickly defeated most of the North Vietnamese forces. The battle for Hue lasted for a month. The siege of Khe Sanh lasted two months.

In response to the Tet Offensive, President Johnson signed Executive Order 11406 on April 10, 1968. The order authorized the Secretary of Defense to order to active duty any unit of the Ready Reserve for a period of not to exceed 24 months. The authorities used for the order came from the Department of Defense Authorization Bill of

---

[58] Lacy, 13-15.

[59] Doubler, 259.

1967 (PL89-687), the same authorities that were used in response to the Pueblo incident. The Secretary of Defense delegated this mobilization authority to the Service Secretaries the following day, subject to these limitations: Army, 20,034; Navy and Marine Corps, 1028; and Air Force, 3488.[60]   A total of 24,500 members of the National Guard and Reserves were mobilized under this order.. Combined with the Pueblo call up, 37,000 reservists were mobilized and available for deployment. The 37, 000 included 500 volunteers and 1600 members of the Individual Ready Reserve that the Army recalled. The Navy called up two Reserve Mobile Construction Battalions, (RMCBs or Seabees) that served seven months in Vietnam. Of the over 9,000 Army Guardsmen from units and individual replacements that served in Vietnam, 7,000 were mobilized in response to the Tet call-up.[61]

The mobilizations of 1968 exposed issues with the reserve forces. The Deputy Assistant Secretary of Defense for Reserve Affairs ordered an internal review. The review found a direct relationship between the full-time support provided reserve units and the readiness levels of the units at the time of mobilization. Units with lower readiness levels took longer to prepare for deployment resulting in less time remaining on their mobilization for deployment. Three observations from the mobilization review stood out. There was a need for better leadership training of noncommissioned officers (NCOs) who had not served on active duty. A more careful selection of units to be

[60] Lacy, 15.

[61] Les' Melnyk, *Mobilizing for the Storm: The Army National Guard in Operations Desert Shield and Desert Storm*, (Alexandria, VA: National Guard Bureau, Historical Services Division, 2001), 8.

mobilized could have avoided certain issues. Units with the higher percentages of

equipment and personnel had a higher overall degree of readiness.[62]

Total Force Policy (Post-Vietnam)

During his second Presidential campaign attempt, Richard Nixon promised to end

the draft. Nixon reasoned that ending the draft would end much of the public and

congressional opposition to the Vietnam War.[63] Shortly after Nixon's election, Secretary

of Defense Laird recommended that the president appoint a commission to determine the

most practical means to eliminate the draft while maintaining a commitment to the

nation's defense.[64] President Nixon established the commission on March 27, 1969 with

former Eisenhower Administration Defense Secretary Thomas S. Gates, Jr. as the

chairman. The committee delivered its final report after eleven months of intensive work

on February 6, 1970. It found that the draft in Vietnam was expensive, divisive and

inequitable for recruiting men. An all-volunteer force could serve as a practical and

desirable alternative to conscription. The committee made three recommendations for an

all-volunteer force: double the base pay for soldiers in their first two years of service,

improve the living conditions and lifestyle of service members and establish a stand-by

draft. The committee also recommended an end to the draft on July 1, 1971.[65]

The National Guard Association of the United States (NGAUS) opposed the

recommendation to end the draft. The draft ensured a steady stream of would-be

---

[62] Lacy, 17.

[63] Congressional Quarterly, *U.S. Draft Policy and Its Impact* (Washington DC: Congressional Quarterly Service, 1968), 7-9, 25-32.

[64] Gus C. Lee and Geoffrey Y. Parker, Ending the Draft-The Story of the All Volunteer Force, Final Report 77-1 (Washington, DC: Department of the Army, April 1977), 37.

[65] Doubler, 273-274.

draftees, joining the National Guard and other reserve forces. NGAUS correctly predicted an end to the draft would sharply reduce the size of the National Guard. NGAUS argued that the draft was cheaper for the American taxpayer. The draft ensured a constant supply of recruits for the reserves. Since the reserves could retain three men on the rolls, for the cost of training a single new recruit, it was cheaper for the reserves to operate during the draft.[66] The Gates Commission report formed the foundation for subsequent reforms under the Nixon administration. These reforms will be discussed in the next chapter.

---

[66] Doubler, 274-275.

CHAPTER 2: NO DRAFT AND THE PERSIAN GULF WAR

It is a Service responsibility to train and equip forces for combat, National Guard and Reserve forces, included. If the Service does not succeed in training its forces, Service readiness suffers as does the Service's relationship with its reserve component forces. The readiness issues of the 1968 mobilizations, an impending end to the draft, looming force reductions, and the public demand for less defense spending, all converged to force a major change in defense policy. Inspired by the Gates Commission report, in 1970 Secretary of Defense Melvin Laird proposed the Total Force Concept. Reserve forces would augment their active duty counterparts to achieve the most cost-effective force mix. In August of 1970, Secretary Laird directed the Services to achieve "economies" by relying on the Guard and Reserve for combat and combat support units. "…to the concurrent consideration of the Total Forces, Active and Reserve….A total force concept will be applied to all aspects of planning, programming, manning, equipping and employing National Guard and Reserve Forces."[1] In his report to Congress in August of 1972, Secretary Laird stated that Pentagon's goal of a volunteer force consisted of "2.3 million Active and 1 million Selected Reserve Members."[2]

The "Abrams Doctrine"

On October 16, 1972, General Creighton Abrams became the Army Chief of Staff. Abrams inherited a plan to reduce the Active Army to 13 divisions and 825,000 personnel, post-Vietnam. This was the smallest the Army had been since before the Korean War. There was discussion of bringing the Army down to eight divisions, with a

---

[1] Secretary of Defense, "Memorandum to the Secretaries of the Military Departments," August 21, 1970.

[2] Secretary of Defense, Report of the Secretary of Defense to the Chairman of the Armed Services Committees: Progress in Ending Draft and Achieving the All Volunteer Force, August 1972, iii.

heavy reliance on nuclear weapons.[3] General Abrams considered a conventional force reduced to that level, would be inadequate to meet the Soviet Threat. Abrams received permission from Laird's successor, Secretary of Defense, James R. Schlesinger, to expand the planned force structure to 16 Active divisions, the force level prior to the build-up for Vietnam, with the provision that the Army would not require additional personnel or equipment.[4] Doing all his own planning, without any input from his staff, Abrams developed a plan to reduce each Active division to two brigades and then designated a Reserve brigade to "roundout" the 16-division structure. Nine Guard brigades would round out nine Active divisions, creating the additional three divisions that Abrams sought, without changing the Active force end strength. On August 22, 1973, following the abolition of the draft, Secretary Schlesinger announced that the Total Force Concept was now the Total Force Policy. He directed the Services to create a "homogenous whole" by increasing the readiness of the reserve components.[5] In March of 1974, General Abrams publicly announced to Congress, the Army's application of the Total Force Concept, first referred to as the "Roundout Strategy." This strategy would later become known as the "Abrams Doctrine."

Under the Roundout Strategy, reserve units would have the same priority for equipment fielding as the active duty counterparts that they would "roundout." The Army permanently assigned roundout brigades to active component divisions for training. The active divisions would have two combat maneuver brigades during

---

[3] Lewis Sorley, Thunderbolt: General Creighton Abrams and the Army of His Time (Bloomington, IN: Indiana University Press, 2008), 362.

[4] Ibid., 363.

[5] Doubler, 278.

peacetime. Upon mobilization, the National Guard combat maneuver brigade would "roundout" the division structure. During peacetime, an Army National Guard (ARNG) brigadier general commanded the roundout brigades. Upon mobilization, the roundout brigade commander would become an assistant division commander. The ARNG would assign a number of combat battalions to active Army divisions to provide a tenth ground maneuver unit to the division structure. By using six roundout brigades and a number of additional ARNG combat maneuver battalions, the Army would be able to reduce the active division structures sufficiently to build three additional divisions.[6]

Proponents of the Abrams Doctrine contend that it served as an additional check on the presidential use of military power. General Abrams was ensuring that there was a "clear linkage between the employment of the Army and the engagement of public support for military operations."[7] General John Vessey, who was serving on the Army Staff at the time, heard General Abrams claim that, "They're not taking us to war again without the Reserves."[8]

Whether General Abrams intended the Roundout Strategy to be an extra-constitutional check on the presidential use of military power or whether he was just trying to save force structure continues to be the subject of much debate. Abrams died in September of 1974; he never published or articulated a specific doctrine. General Vessey, who would later become Chairman of the Joint Chiefs of Staff, was convinced that General Abrams

---

[6] Ibid., 280.

[7] James Carafano, *The Army Reserves and the Abrams Doctrine: Unfulfilled Promise, Uncertain Future* (Washington, DC: Heritage Foundation, 2005), 3-4.

[8] Sorley, "Reserve Components: Looking Back to Look Ahead," *Joint Force Quarterly* 36, (December 2004): 22, http://www.dtic.mil/doctrine/jel/jfq_pubs/0536.pdf (accessed May 30, 2012).

did intend the Roundout Strategy to have a political element.[9] However, in a research paper written by Abrams's son in 1975, Major Abrams argued the decision to implement the Roundout Strategy was driven by force structure requirements. "The basis for the decision was not a carefully worked out staff study, but rather an estimate of the situation – roughly equivalent to a commander's use of the factors of …mission, enemy, terrain and weather, troops available."[10] There was no mention of the Abrams Doctrine in his paper.

Crediting General Abrams with creating an extra-Constitutional check on the employment of the Army discredits his contributions by characterizing the creation of the Roundout Strategy as an unprofessional act, contrary to the professional military ethos described by Samuel P. Huntington. It is more likely that the policy of General Abrams, was addressing the practical challenges of raising 16 divisions, while his comments regarding not going to war without the reserves, merely reflected the opinions of most senior Army officers rather than a political motivation. A survey of general officers who commanded in Vietnam found that 90 percent disapproved of President Johnson's decision not to utilize the Reserves.[11] The common perception at the time was that the draft served a greater deterrent to the presidential use of the military than mobilizing the reserves. The Gates Commission found it necessary to specifically address the notion that an all-volunteer force of active and reserve troops would be less, not more connected, to the American people. The commission argued that there would be little difference

---

[9] Sorley, Thunderbolt, 364

[10] Creighton W. Abrams Jr., "The Sixteen Division Force, Anatomy of a Decision" (Fort Leavenworth, KS: U.S. Army Command and General Staff College, 1975), iii.

[11] Douglas Kinnard, *The War Managers*, 3d. ed. (New York: Da Capo Press, 1991), 117.

between the fundamental nature of a conscription Army and an all-volunteer Army. The commission made a special effort to address a prevalent concern that an all-volunteer force would *not* become further isolated from society.[12] There was a lack of historical perspective for the American people. In every major conflict in U.S. history, the draft had provided a significant source of manpower, so the concept of expanding the military without a draft was completely foreign to the citizens of the United States. The Gates Commission was addressing the concern that a military expanded for war by the reserves would not necessarily be more isolated from the American people than a military expanded by the draft.

In 1975 Secretary Schlesinger began to express doubts with the Total Force Policy. He believed it might have contributed to an over reduction of active ground forces. He advised Congress that, in the aftermath of Vietnam and the changeover to the all-volunteer force, the nation had gone too far in reducing active-duty ground forces.[13] Another criticism was that the new all-volunteer force was "hollow," because both the active and reserve components were below required readiness levels. The "hollow" charge against reserve units did not evoke the same emphasis that it did when leveled against the active forces. Seeing little employment during the war in Vietnam, the majority of Americans viewed the Reserves as a strategic reserve.[14] Secretary Schlesinger's doubts reflected the magnitude of reductions in the Army. In 1968, at the

---

[12] Study, Achieving America's Goals: National Service or the All-Volunteer Armed Force?, Committee on Armed Services, U.S. Senate, February 1977, 44.

[13] Duncan, 144

[14] David R.Segal and Karin De Angelis, "Changing Conceptions of the Military as a Profession," *American Civil Military Relations*, ed. Suzanne C. Nielsen and Don M. Snider (Baltimore, MD: The John Hopkins University Press, 2009), 204.

height of involvement in Vietnam, the regular Army had 1.6 million soldiers. By 1976, active Army end strength was reduced to 775,000.[15]

During the 1980's, increased defense spending produced significant gains in personnel end strength and readiness for active forces, but an inequitable amount of that defense spending found its way to reserve forces. Three separate policy initiatives hindered the readiness in the Reserves in all four Services: Mirror Imaging; First to Fight Funding; and Cascading Modernization.

"Mirror Imaging" held that force structures in the Active components would be "mirrored" by the same type of force structure in the Reserve components. For combat units, if armored brigades were in the Active force, armored brigades would also be in the National Guard. The problem with this was that it required the Guard to retain expensive equipment, without the operating tempo (OPTEMPO) funding to maintain or deploy that equipment. OPTEMPO funding is tied to the estimated annual training mileage for a particular vehicle. OPTEMPO dollars in 1986 were: 800-850 miles for the Active Army, 288-306 for the National Guard, and 200-213 for the Reserves.[16] In 1986, the Army provided three to four times as much funding to the active force to maintain equipment than it provided to the reserve forces for equipment maintenance.

"First to Fight Funding" meant that the Defense Department would first fund those units designated in a war plan as the first to deploy and fight. Because the National Guard and Reserves were follow-on forces in war plans, the Reserves never gained any

---

[15] Doubler, 273.

[16] Congressional Budget Office, *The Army of the Nineties: How Much Will It Cost?* December 1986, (Washington, DC: Government Printing Office, 1986), http://www.cbo.gov/ftpdocs/61xx/doc6188/doc26c-Entire.pdf (accessed January 21, 2012).

priority for funding. Sensing a disparity in equipping the reserve components, in a June 21, 1982 memorandum, Secretary of Defense Weinberger clarified that "units that fight first, be equipped first regardless of component."[17] This clarification gave greater priority to early deploying reserve units, such as the roundout brigades. Reserve unit priority for funding for later deploying units remained well behind active component units.

"Cascading Modernization" called for the active forces to receive the most modern equipment while turning over their outdated equipment to the Reserves.[18] This policy combined with Mirror Imaging and First to Fight Funding contributed to significant differences in the tiered readiness levels between the active and reserve forces throughout the 1980's.

Although funding to equip the reserves lagged behind the active force during Secretary Weinberger's tenure, personnel growth was the opposite. Secretary Weinberger was a strong proponent of the Total Force Policy, as evidenced by his statement to the Congress of the Interallied Confederation of Reserve Officers in August of 1982:

> We can no longer consider reserve forces as merely forces in reserve....Instead they have to be an integral part of the total force, both within the United States and within NATO. They have to be, and in fact are, a blending of the professionalism of the full-time soldier with the professionalism of the citizen-soldier. Only in that way can we achieve the military strength that is necessary to defend our freedom.[19]

---

[17] Caspar Weinberger, Memorandum to the Military Services, "Priorities for Equipment Procurement and Distribution," June 21, 1982.

[18] Carafano, 9.

[19] Edward J. Philbin and James L. Gould, "The Guard and Reserve: In Pursuit of Full Integration," In *The Guard and Reserve in the Total Force*, ed. Bennie J. Wilson III, (Washington, DC: National Defense University Press, 1985), 50.

In a move reminiscent of Secretary McNamara, Secretary Weinberger sought to grow the military at the least possible cost. The goal was to determine the acceptable level of proficiency for tasks within the Department of Defense and select the least costly form of manpower to perform those tasks. That form of manpower was the selected reserves, whereas the most expensive form of manpower was the active force. From 1981 to 1989, active component personnel increased from 2,040,000 to 2,133,000, a growth of less than five percent. During the same timeframe, the selected reserve moved from 869,000 to 1,171,000, an increase of approximately thirty-five percent.[20]

Despite the issues described above, the Total Force Policy did improve funding and readiness levels in the Reserves. Senior leaders in the Reserve Components supported the Abrams Doctrine because it placed increased importance on their mission, secured additional funding, and justified their force structure. The Abrams Doctrine gave far greater relevance to the Reserves than they had enjoyed during the Vietnam era. It was viewed as a dramatic improvement over policies of the President Johnson era. Advocates of the reserve component supported the Abrams Doctrine and the Total Force Policy, even though the effectiveness of both policies had not been tested. The Total Force Policy would not be validated by an involuntary mobilization until 17 years after Secretary of Defense Schlesinger's announcement of the all-volunteer force.[21]

The Total Force Policy during Desert Shield and Desert Storm

The Iraqi army's invasion of Kuwait in 1990 provided the first real test of the Abrams Doctrine. After action reviews of Operation Desert Shield and Desert Storm credit the

---

[20] Duncan, 150-151.

[21] Ibid., 56.

Abrams Doctrine for allowing the Army to effectively take its reserves to war. The Army

mobilized 62,411 soldiers in 398 National Guard units with an additional 1,132

volunteers mobilized for active duty positions. Of those mobilized, 37, 848 deployed to

Southwest Asia and 10, 132 deployed to various locations in the United States to provide

security or to backfill Active units that deployed.[22] The remaining 14, 431 troops or 23

percent of the total National Guard forces mobilized, never deployed to combat or to

support missions.

On August 22, 1990, President George H.W. Bush signed Executive Order 12727, which stated:

> By the authority vested in me as President by the Constitution and the laws of the Unites States of America, including sections 121 and 673(b) of title 10 of the United States Code, I hereby determine that it is necessary to augment the active armed forces of the United States for the effective conduct of operational missions in and around the Arabian Peninsula. Further, under the stated authority, I hereby authorize the Secretary of Defense to order to active duty units of the Selected Reserve.[23]

The Services quickly mobilized National Guard and Reserve Forces before the end of

August (Air Force, 14, 500; Navy, 3000; Marines, 3000; Army 25,000).[24]

The executive power used by President Bush was established by the War Powers Act

of 1973. The Presidential Selective Reserve Call-up (PRSC) gives the president the

authority to mobilize up to 200,000 reservists from units of the Ready Reserve for 90

days with the option to extend the call-up for an additional 90 days. In 1976, Congress

passed a new statute giving the president authority to call-up reservists for a short period,

---

[22] Melnyk, 2.

[23] John Woolley and Gerhard Peters, *The American Presidency Project*, "Executive Order 12727 - Ordering the Selected Reserve of the Armed Forces to Active Duty," August 22, 1990, http://www.presidency.ucsb.edu/ws/index.php?pid=23568#ixzz1khQFb9q3http://www.presidency.ucsb.edu/ws/index.php?pid=23568#axzz1khPOl4LE (accessed January 21, 2012).

[24] Brian Harris. *Relevance of Army National Guard Infantry Units in the Force Structure and Their Role in Combat*, (Carlisle Barracks, PA: U.S. Army War College, 2004): 7, http://www.dtic.mil/cgi-bin/GetTRDoc?AD=ADA423614&Location=U2&doc=GetTRDoc.pdf (accessed May 30, 2012).

without seeking congressional approval. Section 673b allowed the president to call to active duty up to 200,000 reservists for up to 180 days.[25] Had President Bush initially chosen a partial mobilization of the reserves, this would have obligated reservists for up to one year. A partial mobilization would have required congressional approval for any overseas commitment of troops into a combat situation within sixty days or could have been challenged outright by Congress. Since the situation with Iraq was uncertain at the time, President Bush used his PRSC authority, with the option of later going to Congress for authority to extend the period of mobilization, should the need dictate. This was the first time since Vietnam that an American President had involuntarily activated reservists.[26]

The Secretary of Defense, Richard Cheney, informed the Services how many and what type of units each Service could activate. Based on senior Army input from his own staff, Secretary Cheney directed the Army to mobilize only combat support and combat service support units, not combat units. He did not place similar restrictions on any of the other Services.

Although the Army had matched roundout brigades with active divisions that would be among the first to deploy in case of war, the Army had never intended to deploy the roundout brigades or other reserve combat units in a short-term situation unless it involved the Soviet Union or a full mobilization. A Government Accountability Office (GAO) report to Congress in 1988 concluded that the Army planned to deploy active component divisions with active component brigades, not the roundout brigades. The

---

[25] Doubler, 284.

[26] Duncan, 19.

Department of the Army did not intend the roundout brigades to accompany the initial deploying active divisions. The roundout brigades would be part of reinforcements that would arrive 30 to 90 days after commencement of combat.[27] This policy differed substantially from what the Army publicly discussed with the National Guard. The decision to exclude Guard combat units from the call-up came as quite a surprise to the National Guard. The Army saw the situation differently than the National Guard which was anxious to prove the capabilities of the roundout brigades.

The Army viewed the initial deployment to the Gulf as too uncertain to mobilize the roundout brigades. In August of 1990, the situation with Iraq was tenuous. Iraq could have withdrawn from Kuwait. Since Army leadership had been criticized for calling up the reserves for apparently no reason during the Berlin crisis, it had no desire to relive that criticism by mobilizing combat units that it did not intend to deploy to the Persian Gulf.[28]

The Army's first active duty units received their deployment orders on August 6, 1990, The 24th Infantry Division, stationed at Fort Stewart, Georgia was the Army's first heavy division to deploy. Its roundout unit was the 48th Infantry Brigade (Mechanized) from the Georgia Army National Guard. Instead of mobilizing the 48th Brigade to roundout the 24th Infantry Division, the Army selected the 197th Infantry Brigade which supported training at the Army's Infantry School at Fort Benning, Georgia. Unlike the 24th Infantry Division and its roundout, the 48th Brigade, which were

---

[27]Government Accountability Office, *National Guard Peacetime Training did not Adequately Prepare Combat Brigades for Gulf War: Report to the Secretary of the Army* (Washington, DC: Government Printing Office, 1991): 10, http://archive.gao.gov/d19t9/144875.pdf (accessed January 23, 2012).

[28] Robert L. Goldich, *The Army's Roundout Concept After the Persian Gulf War* (Washington, DC: Congressional Research Service, Library of Congress, October 22,1991), 11.

equipped with the Army's latest M-1 Abrams Main Battle Tanks and M-2 Bradley Fighting Vehicles, the 197th Brigade had M60 Battle Tanks and M113 Armored Personnel Carriers. The Army had also sent deployment orders to the 1st Cavalry Division at Fort Hood, Texas. Its roundout unit was the 155th Armored Brigade from the Mississippi Army National Guard. Instead of mobilizing the 155th Brigade, the Army chose to augment the 1st Cavalry Division with the 1st Brigade of the 2d Armored Division. Although the choice to augment the 24th Infantry Division with the 197th Brigade and the 1st Cavalry Division with the 1st Brigade of the 2d Armored Division may have seemed inconsistent with the roundout policy, it spoke to a much larger problem of the Army's inability to communicate to Congress and the National Guard its policy for utilizing the roundout brigades.

When President Bush announced the call-up of the Reserves, he set off a bureaucratic storm in the Pentagon as the various Services began nominating reserve units for mobilizations. The first Service estimates came back with 300,000 troops, which exceeded the president's authority by 100,000 troops and was bigger than the entire planned force for Desert Shield. General Powell, the Chairman of the Joint Chiefs of Staff, directed General Schwarzkopf, the Commander in Chief (CINC) who would be commanding the forces in theater, to select the forces that would be mobilized. The Goldwater-Nichols legislation gave General Schwarzkopf new authorities as CINC; he would be able to pick and choose the forces that he wanted deployed to the Gulf.[29] Having the best sense of what was needed for the fight, General Schwarzkopf wanted troops from the Reserves to take on the tasks of supporting the deployment: stevedores,

---

[29] Duncan, 37.

ammunition handlers, telephone installers, truck drivers and mechanics. The Chief of

Staff of the Army, General Vuono tried to convince General Schwarzkopf to take the

roundout brigades in order to prove the Army's concept worked. General Vuono was

also under political pressure from congressional leaders from the states with the roundout

brigades. General Schwarzkopf refused because it made no sense to accept roundout

units for at most 180 days when so much time was needed for getting the units trained for

war. General Powell supported General Schwarzkopf's decision.[30]

Behind the scenes, Senator Sam Nunn from Georgia and Senator Sonny Montgomery

of Mississippi, both members of the Senate Armed Services Committee, along with

congressmen on the House Armed Services Committee, put pressure on Secretary

Cheney to mobilize the roundout brigades from their respective states (48th Infantry

Brigade from Georgia and the 155th Armored Brigade from Mississippi). In a letter dated

September 6, 1990 the Chairman of the House Armed Services Committee, Les Aspin

wrote:

> …Why, for example when the 24th Infantry Division at Fort Stewart, Georgia, was mobilized, wasn't its Army National Guard round-out brigade (the 48th Infantry Brigade) activated as well? Why wasn't the 155th Armored Brigade in Mississippi called up with the First Cav?
> In Operation Desert Shield, the Department of Defense has a unique opportunity to test the reserve system, generally, and the validity of the active component's concerns about the need for refresher training for reserve combat units, more specifically. We recognize that there is considerable resistance within the active component to utilizing the reserves for combat missions. Active duty generals want to command infantrymen and tank crews, not supply sergeants and truck drivers. Yet, given increased warning times, we may in the future wish to place far more combat capability in the reserve and guard, while maintaining a broad combat support and combat service support base in the active forces. According to the Government Accountability Office analysis, many combat skills in fact, require far less training time to maintain proficiency than combat support and

---

[30] Norman H. Schwarzkopf, *It Doesn't Take a Hero*, (New York: Bantam Books, 1992), 377.

combat service support skills and are, therefore, particularly well-suited for assignment to the reserves.[31]

Secretary Cheney responded by letter to Representative Les Aspin. In his response, Cheney stated that he had not authorized the call-up of Army combat units because his senior military advisors had not advised him that their call-up was necessary. They were concerned that too much of the 180-day statutory time limit would be consumed by preparation, pre-deployment training, and transportation to and from the Middle East. Therefore the Reserve forces could not be stationed in the region for a full rotation period.[32] Secretary Cheney neglected to mention the timing of the deployment orders. When the 24th Infantry Division received its deployment orders on August 6, the only option available to the Army for deploying a third brigade to augment the 24th was to select an active duty unit. President Bush did not authorize the call-up of any reserve forces until August 22, sixteen days later.[33]

By the end of October, 1990 most of the forces for Operation Desert Storm had closed on the Persian Gulf. On October 24, Congress adopted an amendment to the House (Defense) Appropriations Bill:

> Sec. 8132. During fiscal year 1991, in exercising the authority provided…under section 673b of Title 10, … The president may use that authority in the case of orders to active duty in support of operations in and around the Arabian Peninsula and Operation Desert Shield as if "180 days" were substituted for "90 days"… Provided, that this section only applies to Selected Reserve combat Units.[34]

---

[31]Les Aspin, Letter to the Secretary of Defense, Richard B. Cheney, September 6, 1990.

[32] Letter, Secretary Cheney to Chairman Aspin, September 18, 1990 reply to 6 Sep 90 letter from committee members Les Aspin GV Montgomery, Beverly Byron and Dave McCurdy.

[33] Doubler, 312.

[34] Conference Report (to accompany H.R. 5803), Making Appropriations for the Department of Defense, Report 101-938, House of Representatives, One Hundred First Congress, Second Session, October 24, 1990.

The defense of Saudi Arabia had proven successful but to expel Saddam Hussein from Kuwait, additional forces would be needed for offensive capabilities. On October 30, 1990, President Bush asked King Fahd and coalition leaders to approve offensive action against Iraqi forces occupying Kuwait.[35] On November 8, 1990, the president ordered additional troops to the Persian Gulf to include the Army's VII Corps in Europe and the 1st Infantry Division from Fort Riley, Kansas. In addition to these forces, the Army mobilized five National Guard heavy combat brigades: the 48th Infantry Brigade (Mechanized), the 155th Armored Brigade, the 256th Infantry Brigade (Mechanized), and the 142d and 196th Field Artillery Brigades. Roundout battallions that provided the tenth maneuver battalion to their divisions, received their mobilization orders as well. The 1-263d Armor Battalion from South Carolina would train with the 48th Brigade from Georgia to roundout the 24th Infantry Division. The 3-141st Infantry Battalion from Texas would train with the 155th Brigade from Mississippi to augment the 1st Cavalry Division and the 2-152d Armor Battalion from Alabama would train with the 256th Infantry Brigade.[36] Both the 2-152 Armor Battalion and the 256th Infantry Brigade were roundouts for the 5th Infantry Division, but the 5th Infantry Division was not slated for deployment to the Persian Gulf.

U.S. troop build-up escalated rapidly, once President Bush had committed to offensive action in November. UN Resolution 678, established January 15, 1991 for Saddam Hussein to withdraw his forces from Kuwait. On November 1, there were 91 mobilized Army National Guard units with 9,102 soldiers. On December 15, there were 301 units

---

[35] Duncan, 68.

[36] Doubler, 314-316.

with 50,041 mobilized Army National Guard soldiers. While about 40,000 of these members of the National Guard were still at mobilization stations, by the January 15 deadline, some 23,000 members were in the Persian Gulf.[37]

On November 30, the 48th Infantry Brigade and the 256th Infantry Brigade reached their mobilization stations at Fort Stewart, Georgia and Fort Polk, Louisiana, respectively. Upon arrival, both units learned their current level of training was immaterial to planned post-mobilization training. All training would have to begin at the most basic tasks and progress accordingly.[38] Army Active component trainers notified the units that they were not competent to train themselves or evaluate their own level of training. Training would begin as if the units had just entered the Army, without any prior training. The unit would receive additional training to include obstacle breaching and counter-reconnaissance training in order to receive combat certification.[39] The Active Army with less than forty percent of its force structure deployed to the Persian Gulf, had sufficient capacity to train and evaluate National Guard forces. As mentioned previously, the 5th Infantry Division, of which the 256th Infantry Brigade was a roundout for, was not deploying to the Persian Gulf.

After a few day of medical screening, in-processing and individual training, the 48th Infantry Brigade deployed to the National Training Center (NTC) at Fort Irwin, California. The 256th Infantry Brigade deployed to Fort Polk, Louisiana for New Equipment Training (NET), to transition from M60 tanks and M113 personnel carriers to

---

[37] Melnyk, 15.

[38] For a differing opinion see GAO "National Guard Peacetime Training did not Adequately Prepare Combat Units for Gulf War). http://archive.gao.gov/d19t9/144875.pdf (accessed January 23, 2012).

[39] Melnyk, 18.

M1 Abrams main battle tanks. The 155th Armored Brigade deployed to Fort Hood, Texas.

Because there had been so much previous attention focused on why the Army had not mobilized combat units, significant national media attention followed these units on their odyssey to earn combat certification. Leadership was the first issue highlighted. Many leaders lacked either requisite schooling or experience. A large number of noncommissioned officers lacked professional schooling for the positions that they held. Prior to mobilization, the Army Mobilization and Planning System (AMOPS) required noncommissioned officers to be qualified in their occupational specialties, in order to be deployable. Now, the AMOPS standards were replaced with Active Army standards. This required noncommissioned officers to have completed requisite leadership schooling in addition to being qualified in their occupational schooling to hold a leadership position. Eight company commanders from the 256th were relieved for inability to deal with stress.[40] Although the reasons are not specified, the commander of Second Army, then BG Wesley Clark, relieved the commander of the 48th Brigade, BG William Holland. When asked to comment, MAJ John Wagstaffe, a spokesman for BG Clark stated that BG Holland was not relieved. "To my knowledge, he wasn't relieved. The Georgia governor and adjutant general said they desperately needed him in Georgia to command another unit." MAJ Wagstaffe also denied that Active Army leadership was trying to subvert the leadership of the National Guard chain of command. According to Wagstaffe, there was only one instance where a regular Army officer was inserted into

---

[40] Ibid., 20.

45

the 48th Brigade - that was to replace the deputy commander when the deputy commander (COL James D. Davis) replaced BG Holland as the commander.[41]

Maintenance issues plagued the 48th Brigade. The Army decided to field a new automated logistics system for maintenance, Unit Level Logistics System, Ground (ULLS-G) when the 48th arrived at the National Training Center. This made maintaining the equipment at the National Training Center particularly difficult. The maintenance personnel were in classrooms learning the new system while their units were in a field environment struggling to maintain equipment without them.[42]

An embarassing incident for the Army National Guard occurred when 53 soldiers from Louisiana's 256th Brigade went AWOL from training after the unit moved to Fort Hood. The unit moved from to Fort Polk to Fort Hood in January of 1991 to complete platoon and company sized maneuver training on the M-1 tank and M-2 Bradley Fighting Vehicle. These soldiers went AWOL in February. While absent from Fort Hood the soldiers complained to local media about the poor living conditions, poor food, broken promises about time off, and that central Texas was cold and muddy. Two days after going AWOL, 40 of the soldiers returned to Fort Hood.[43] The 256th Brigade expected the remaining 13 soldiers to return shortly thereafter. Eventually, all but one of the soldiers

---

[41] Kenneth Reich, "Call-up and Non-deployment of Southern Guard Units Spark Furor: Troops: Their Readiness Was Questioned. Georgia's 48th Brigade trained in the California desert at Ft. Irwin--and then trained some more. Political issues are raised." *L.A. Times*. March 08, 1991, http://articles.latimes.com/1991-03-08/news/mn-2584_1_desert-training (accessed January 25, 2012).

[42] Melnyk, 20.

[43] Louis Sahagun and John Broder,. "40 AWOL Guardsmen Come Back : Reserves: Members of a Louisiana unit return to their posts in Texas, two days after leaving. They will face military charges." *L.A. Times*, February 8, 1991, http://articles.latimes.com/keyword/national-guard-u-s (accessed January 25, 2012).

returned on their own from Shreveport, Louisiana to face non-judicial punishment.[44] Their complaints failed to evoke public sympathy, since there was a war going on in the Persian Gulf at the time. Their efforts did demonstrate significant morale and discipline problems in the roundout brigades, while also embarrassing Army leadership.

After 91 days from the beginning of their mobilization, BG Wesley Clark certified the 48th Brigade as combat-ready. This ended the longest rotation at the National Training Center on record.[45] The 91 days (51 of those days were at the National Training Center), included 15 days lost to transit and 30 days of additional training on assaulting Iraqi-style defensive positions. The 46 remaining training days (not spent in transit or additional training) exceeded the 42 days previously recommended prior to Desert Shield by the Commanding General of the 24th Infantry Division and reviewed by the Commander of Forces Command, the Army's Deputy Chief of Staff for Operations and the Chief of Staff of the Army.[46] On February 28, 1991, the same day that the ground war ended for Operation Desert Storm, the 48th Brigade was officially ready for combat.

The irony in BG Wes Clark certifying the 48th Brigade ready for combat is not that it happened the same day that the war ended. The irony is that the 48th Brigade completed a rotation at the National Training Center in July of 1990. At the conclusion of that rotation, BG Clark noted that the 48th had, "performed as well or better than most active units that have come through."[47] BG Clark's comparison of the 48th Brigade performing as well or better than most active units at the National Training Center emphasizes the

---

[44] Doubler, 317.

[45] Ibid., 315.

[46] Melnyk, 19, 21.

[47] Doubler, 331.

Army's failure to identify significant readiness issues in leader development, maintenance training and discipline during a peacetime rotation. BG Clark's peacetime assessment was most likely inflated or the 48th Brigade would not have required so much training just six months later.

In contrast to the experiences of the three roundout brigades, two Army National artillery brigades transitioned easily from mobilization station to deployment to the Persian Gulf. The 196th Field Artillery Brigade from Tennessee, Kentucky and West Virginia trained under field conditions for one week to validate collective training and then conducted a three-day command post exercise before shipping their equipment overseas to Saudi Arabia. The brigade was in Saudi Arabia two months after mobilization and fired its first mission less than three weeks later. The 142d Field Artillery Brigade from Arkansas and Oklahoma shipped its equipment to Saudi Arabia three weeks after mobilization and closed on Saudi Arabia one month later. The 196th Brigade was in theater eight weeks following deployment, while the 142d Brigade was in theater seven weeks after deployment.[48] Both units performed extremely well during Operation Desert Storm, proving that reserve component combat brigades could deploy on time and fight as designed. The Army did not insist the artillery brigades replace AMOPS standards with Active Army standards for leadership training. The Army did not apply the same deployment standards it required for the roundout brigades to other deploying forces.

The U.S. Air Force and its Tactical Air Command (TAC) viewed the impending war in the Persian Gulf as an opportunity to prove that the Air Force Reserve and Air

---

[48] Melnyk, 22-23.

National Guard units could integrate and perform as well during wartime as during peacetime. The 706th Tactical Fighter Squadron (TFS) from New Orleans, Louisiana made history as the first Air Force Reserve unit to execute combat missions. The 706th had A-10A Thunderbolt II aircraft, armed with a 30mm cannon. The aircraft were also capable of carrying six 500-pound bombs, cluster bombs and air-to-air missiles. The Air Force was anxious to get rid of the A-10 airplanes in favor of faster, more technologically advanced jets like the F-16, but the A-10 proved to be very effective against Iraqi tanks and SCUD missile launchers.[49]

The 706th TFS was one of the premier units in the Air Force Reserve. It was part of the 926th Tactical Fighter Group (TFG), which had received the Air Force outstanding unit award. The commander, Colonel Bob Efferson, was a former Vietnam F-105 pilot. Colonel Efferson had claimed that his unit was at such a state of readiness, that it could deploy anywhere in the world three days after receiving its mobilization orders. Given its deployment orders on December 29, 1990, his unit had the chance to prove his claim. By January 1, 1991, all eighteen aircraft from the 706th had arrived in the Gulf. By January 5th, the aviation support package including elements of the 926th Consolidated Aviation Support Squadron and additional staff and support personnel from the 926th TFG arrived in Saudi Arabia. Over one-third, or 450 of 1200 personnel assigned to the 926th TFG deployed to the Gulf in one week or less.[50]

By January 17, 1991, crews from the 926th were flying armed reconnaissance missions against the Iraqi Army and would continue doing so for fifty-two days, until a cease-fire

---

[49] Duncan, 94-95.

[50] Ibid., 96.

took effect. Pilots from the 926th flew over 1,000 missions without losing a single pilot or aircraft. One of the 706th pilots downed an Iraqi helicopter, the first-ever air-to-air kill by an A-10. Two A-10 pilots working in tandem destroyed twenty SCUD launchers, ammunition warehouses plus other targets in one day. Despite 378 holes in his airplane from Iraqi 57mm antiaircraft rounds, Colonel Efferson still managed to fly his A-10 back to base.[51]

The success of the 926th is directly attributable to the high levels of readiness the unit maintained during peacetime. The Air Force was committed to proving that its reserve units could integrate and perform well during wartime. Colonel Effinginton was a combat veteran of Vietnam anxious to be part of the first Air Force Reserve fighter squadron in history to participate in combat. He encouraged members of his unit to be as ready as possible by validating wills, powers of attorneys, child custody arrangements and other personal matters as early as late August and early September against the contingency that the 926th TFG would get the call.[52]

In contrast to the difficulties the Army experienced in training the roundout brigades, the Marine Corps demonstrated little difficulty in training its reserve combat units. The Marine Corps had been adamant that it would not need any support from the Marine Reserves for the first sixty days of a contingency operation. Once the president and the coalition decided to prepare for offensive operations, the Marines opted to call-up their reserves. On November 6, 1990 the Marine Corps was the first Service to announce mobilizing reserve combat forces – two days before the Army announced it would

---

[51] Duncan, 96-97.
[52] Ibid., 94-95.

mobilize roundout brigades. The Marine Corps mobilized B and D tank companies, 4th Tank Battalion, 4nd Marine Division, from the Marine Reserve, equipped with M60A3 tanks. Several weeks before the mobilization order, the Marines had decided that Marine tank crews would be more survivable if they transitioned to the M-1 Abrams tank than in the M60A3 tanks. Both reserve companies would have to transition to the newer M-1 tank days before deploying to Saudi Arabia. This would significantly shorten the available training timeline for training on combat skills and for new equipment training. The companies would also have to reorganize and fight as three platoons with four tanks each, rather than two platoons with five tanks, each. On December 15, 1990, B Company had official mobilization orders. Two days later, B Company arrived at Twenty-nine Palms Marine Corps training base in California to begin intensive training over the Christmas holiday period. On January 17, 1991, B Company arrived in Saudi Arabia for final training. Some of the training included breaching operations to deal with the massive obstacle belts emplaced by the Iraqi Army over the period of several months, consisting of mines, wire and tank ditches. Prior to the ground war, other activities included tactical movement training, crew drills and vehicle maintenance.[53]

B Company validated its training readiness by its performance in combat. The ground war commenced at H-Hour, 0400 hours on February 24, 1991. B Company crossed into Kuwait at 0458 hours. By 1445 hours B Company had breached two minefields and was in direct fire engagements with the Iraqi Army. The company spent much of the next twelve hours dealing with 396 Iraqi prisoners. It was not until 0200 hours on the 25th of

---

[53] Ibid., 98.

February, that B Company moved into a laager position with 360-degree security, for some much needed rest.

A half hour before sunrise, some men in the company thought they heard what sounded like enemy tank engines. A scan through the M-1s thermal sights confirmed what the Marines heard. There were at least twelve T-72 tanks headed right for B Company's position. A brief but fierce battle ensued. Within seven minutes, B Company's thirteen tanks destroyed over thirty enemy vehicles. The battle lasted another fifteen minutes with a few more enemy vehicles destroyed. When daylight arrived, the company was able to fully understand the extent of the battle. B Company had made contact with an Iraqi tank battalion, reinforced by two mechanized infantry battalions. B Company destroyed thirty T-72 tanks, four T-55 tanks and seven armored personnel carriers. The Iraqi column had been on its way to attack a Marine supply convoy when it bumped into B Company, 4th Tank Battalion, 4nd Marine Division, U.S. Marine Corps Reserve.[54]

Operation Desert Storm highlighted the success and failure of Service policies for integrating their reserve components. The Air Force had successfully maintained a high training readiness rate in its reserve component forces; the Air Force deployed and integrated an A-10 squadron into the Persian Gulf three days after receipt of its mobilization order. The Marine Corps had claimed that it could operate for sixty days of a contingency operation before needing the Marine Reseve. The Marine Corps successfully kept its reserve forces at a high training readiness rate. After operating for

---

[54]US Navy Desert Storm chronology, DEPARTMENT OF THE NAVY - NAVAL HISTORICAL CENTER http://www.history.navy.mil/wars/dstorm/dsfeb.htm (accessed January 17, 2012). ; Duncan, 98-99.

sixty days in the Gulf, the Marines requested to mobilize two reserve tank companies. Two days after receipt of mobilization orders, its tank companies arrived at 29 Palms for training. One month later, those tank companies had transitioned to M-1 tanks, trained for combat and arrived in the Persian Gulf. The Army did not maintain the same training readiness rate in its roundout brigades that the Air Force and Marines did in their reserve combat units. BG Clark certified the first roundout brigade ready for combat 91 days after receipt of its mobilization order. The units never deployed to Iraq.

Operation Desert Storm became the first war in American history that did not include ground maneuver units from the reserve components of the Army. The Army's arguments against using the roundout brigades are not particularly cogent because the Army leadership never seriously considered employing the roundouts for the Gulf War.[55] Necessity forced the decision to mobilize the roundout brigades. If the Army faced a protracted ground war with Iraq, then the roundouts could deploy as reinforcements. If the United States faced another regional conflict, such as Korea, then the roundouts would be trained and ready as a strategic reserve to deploy accordingly.[56] Much of the active component strategic reserve ground forces stationed in the United States and Germany had already deployed to the Gulf as part of Desert Shield. At no time during the mobilization period for the roundouts did the Army allocate or even plan for ship space or airframes to move the roundouts to the Gulf. The Army did not share this omission with the roundouts, with National Guard leadership, or with Congress. It would have been a substantial blow to the morale of the roundout brigades to inform them that

---

[55] Doubler, 312-313.

[56] Ibid., 314.

the intensive training they were involved in was to prepare them for a better-trained calling in the strategic reserve. At a meeting on December 12, 1990 Secretary of Defense Cheney opined that the Army opposed using the roundout brigades because it was "politically correct" to use the roundout brigades..[57] The argument that it takes too long to train National Guard combat units for a war did not apply to the 196th and 142 Field Artillery Brigades, although training combat units that have to maneuver does take additional time. The Marine Corps proved its ability to train combat maneuver units and field new equipment to two Marine Corps Reserve tank companies that distinguished themselves well in combat. It does take longer to train companies than entire brigades, but the Army did not appear anxious to deploy the roundout brigades. It is likely that the Army's unspoken decision to not employ the roundout brigades was motivated by the same rationale that began the program in the first place – saving active component force structure. General Abrams wanted sixteen divisions in the Army and saw the roundout brigades as a means to achieve that goal at no additional cost in force structure. The Army was losing active component force structure before the Gulf War began. If the Army utilized the roundout brigades during Operation Desert Storm and those brigades performed well, the Army would have demonstrated to Congress that there was a less expensive alternative to active component heavy brigades.

The lead-up to the Gulf War marked the first time that American forces might encounter large-scale tank battles since World War II. The Army was losing active component structure even as the build-up in the Persian Gulf progressed. The active strength of the Army was 765,287 at the beginning of fiscal year 1990 on October 1,

---

[57] Duncan, 80.

1989. Exactly one year later, the Army active force numbered 728,252. At the beginning of fiscal year 1992, Army active component end strength waned to 706,160. From the year prior to the build-up in the Persian Gulf, through the conclusion of Operations Desert Shield and Desert Storm the Army lost over 59,000 authorizations, which represented almost eight percent of its force. During the next six fiscal years the Army was slated to lose an additional 200,000 soldier and civilian authorizations.[58] Even though the Army had used the roundout concept to help its lobby for new equipment such as M-1 Abrams tanks and M-2 Bradley Fighting Vehicles, employing roundout brigades in combat would run counter to the Army's struggle to retain active component force structure. If roundout brigades deployed and performed well in combat, then the Army would have difficulty trying to justify keeping its active force structure. Since less than forty percent of the active Army participated in Operation Desert Storm, had National Guard maneuver combat forces deployed and proven themselves as a viable expeditionary force, it is possible that the Army might have found itself trying to convince Congress not to cut additional forces. Had the roundout brigades proven themselves in the Gulf War, Congress would have an alternative that was less expensive than active heavy maneuver brigades.[59]

More Mobilization Authority

By early January 1991, it had become increasingly clear that the Services had manpower requirements exceeding the mobilization authority of the Presidential

---

[58] Department of the Army Historical Summary: FYs 1990 & 1991. http://www.history.army.mil/books/DAHSUM/1990-91/ch03.htm (accessed January 18, 2012). Active Army end strength was programmed to meet 580,000 by the end of FY 97.

[59] With the concurrence from Secretary Cheney, the Army could have activated the roundouts for training, outside the mobilization window, if the Army really needed to employ the brigades in the Persian Gulf.

Selective Reserve Call-up. The PRSC only gave the Services access to the Selected

Reserve within the Ready Reserve. There were skills and experience that did not exist in

units of the Selected Reserve but did exist in former members of the military who had not

completed their service obligation and were therefore assigned to the Individual Ready

Reserve. The president needed to order a partial mobilization to activate those individuals

with unique skills and qualifications not found in the Selected Reserve but required as

individual replacements. On January 16, 1991, President Bush announced initial air

strikes against Iraq as the beginning of the liberation of Kuwait. He authorized the

Department of Defense to call any member of the Ready Reserve, not part of a unit, to

active duty not to exceed twenty-four consecutive months.[60]

Reforms after the Persian Gulf War

The ground war portion of Operation Desert Storm lasted less than five days. On

February 28, 1991 President Bush ordered a cease-fire. The U.S. military did not get a

chance to test many of the systems and policies required for a sustained war because the

ground war was so short. The Gulf War demonstrated that the Total Force Policy, if

applied wisely could be both effective and efficient. The all-volunteer force and every

Service demonstrated effectiveness by rapidly deploying forces with substantial speed

and numbers to deter the Iraqi forces from attacking Saudi Arabia. The Total Force

Policy effectively augmented the active component forces with trained and ready reserve

component forces required to quickly win the war. The Total Force Policy proved its

efficiency by providing savings to the American taxpayer as a result of the reduced cost

of a smaller active military capable of being expanded by trained reserve forces.

---

[60] Duncan, 89.

The policy reforms following Operation Desert Shield aimed at making the Total Force Policy even better. The all-volunteer force had proven better educated and disciplined than the draft-dependent force during Vietnam. The Air Force and Marines demonstrated great success with training and employing combat forces. The peacetime training of the Army's roundout brigades did not prepare those units adequately for their wartime mission and the professional development of many of the leaders in the roundout brigades lagged behind their active counterparts.

The end of Operation Desert Storm foreshadowed the end for the roundout brigades. By not deploying the 48th Infantry Brigade and 155th Armored Brigade with their roundout divisions, the Army admitted that the roundout concept would not work as previously touted. The Army began to focus on rapidly deploying forces from the continental United States (CONUS) instead of relying on the more expensive alternative of forward stationing of troops. The need to project forces rapidly from CONUS and the outdated roundout policy coalesced into a "roundup" program. Under the "roundup" program the Army would have five, full-strength, active force divisions assigned to a contingency corps, capable of rapidly deploying for worldwide operations. Roundup brigades would follow their parent divisions later as reinforcements. By 1992, the 24th Infantry Division and the 1st Cavalry Division each had three active component brigades assigned. The 48th and 155th Brigades became roundup brigades to each division, respectively. The Army did retain five National Guard brigades as roundout brigades with their pre-Desert Shield parent divisions. The roundup program signaled a shift in Army policy towards relying less on the reserve component for immediate deployment to war. Critics of the Army's new roundup program saw it as a poorly veiled effort to save active component force structure.[61]

Another lesson from the Gulf War was the realization of the Services that 90 days extendable for another 90 days was insufficient time for the reserve components to effectively participate in overseas missions. A burgeoning of peacekeeping and humanitarian assistance missions overseas convinced senior military leadership to petition Congress for additional authority under 673b of the Presidential Selective Reserve Call-up. Congress responded by extending the president's authority to 270 days.[62]

In spite of the overall successes of reserve component units that participated in the Gulf War, much of the political memory of Congress focused on the three roundout brigades that never deployed. Congress instituted minor reforms to enhance the overall readiness and deployability of the reserve component.   The Army National Guard Reform Act of 1992 carried over to Title XI of the 1993 Defense Authorization Act. Congress authorized as many as 5,000 active component soldiers for assignment to National Guard units in order to improve readiness and training. The legislation prescribed limiting post-mobilization training time by increasing active component engagement with training assistance and training oversight during peacetime.[63]

The Army responded to congressional persuasion by introducing the "Bold Shift," initiative, which assigned 1300 Regulars, or active component soldiers, to the roundout

---

[61] Doubler, 334.

[62] U.S. Congress, Public Law 103-337, October 5, 1994.

[63] Doubler, 337

and roundup brigades as advisors and training evaluators. The intent of Bold Shift was to use Title XI personnel to improve leader and staff training, focus higher quality training at the individual and lower unit levels and institute operational readiness evaluations to gauge readiness and the ability to deploy quickly.

The end of the Gulf War coincided with other major worldwide events. German reunification and the fall of the Soviet Union spurred reform-minded politicians to call for the peace dividend. In 1992, Governor Bill Clinton pledged a new era of less defense spending in his successful challenge to defeat President Bush. Following his inauguration, President Clinton chose Representative Les Aspin, former chairman of the House Armed Services Committee, as his Secretary of Defense. A long-time critic of the Pentagon, Secretary Aspin initiated a "Bottom-Up Review" (BUR) to address a new U.S. strategy in the post-Cold War era.[64]

The BUR envisioned the U.S. military having to fight two regional conflicts, simultaneously. The active Army was shrinking to 10 divisions, which only provided enough forces to win one regional conflict. National Guard combat forces would reinforce active forces in one conflict and deter or possibly fight the second regional conflict alone. Secretary Aspin vowed to make the Guard combat units better trained, more ready and more capable than ever before. At a press briefing on September 1, 1993, Secretary Aspin announced that the Army National Guard would provide 15 "enhanced readiness brigades" as part of the nation's defense. Enhanced brigades would have priority for personnel, new equipment and training resources. The enhanced brigades were to be able to deploy to a combat zone within 90 days of mobilization. The BUR

---

[64] Ibid., 348-349.

introduced the enhanced brigades and ended the roundup and roundout programs at the

same time.[65]

_____

[65] Ibid., 349-351.

CHAPTER 3: U.S. MILITARY AT WAR AFTER 9-11

The Clinton Administration frequently employed the U.S. military thoughout the 1990's in a variety of operations. Military forces conducted peacekeeping operations in Somalia, Haiti, Bosnia and Herzegovina, and the Sinai. Riots in Los Angeles after the Rodney King verdict, Hurricane Andrew, the Great Flood of 1998 on the Mississippi and the 1996 Olympics tested the military's domestic response capability. The military also supported counter-drug operations and advisory roles for foreign militaries in Central and South America. All of these missions kept military forces busy, but did little to enhance combat readiness.[1] Following terrorist attacks on September 11, 2001, the U.S. military found itself in a new era with plenty of opportunities to improve training and combat readiness.

With the U.S. invasion of Afghanistan, followed less than two years later by the invasion of Iraq, the U.S. military soon experienced the first sustained conflict since Vietnam but without the pool of manpower the draft had provided. The Army was much smaller than it had been during the Vietnam conflict and struggled with the challenges of continuously providing forces for combat. As the conflict stretched into a multi-year endeavor with no end in sight, the Services made adjustments to force generation and training. The continued demands for forces in support of operations in Iraq and Afghanistan exceeded the capability of the Services, especially the Army and Marines, to provide all the forces being asked for by combatant commanders. The Persian Gulf War had not lasted long enough to be considered a sustained conflict. Therefore there had

---

[1] Doubler, 352-360.

been no need for force rotation policies during Desert Shield or Desert Storm. As a result, the Army's capability to deliver forces had not been stressed.

In response to an overcommitment of its forces in the Global War on Terrorism and to facilitate a more predictable and reliable means to provide forces for combat, the Army borrowed heavily on the Air Force's force generation model. In 2006, The secretary of the Army approved the Army Force Generation (ARFORGEN) model. Instead of having a tiered readiness system in which the first forces to deploy had the highest levels of personnel, equipment and training, the ARFORGEN process applies readiness across the entire force, both active and reserve. Each unit would have three periods of readiness: one period when the unit was training for combat; one period when the unit was deployed or readily available for deployment; and one period when it was resetting to begin training again.[2] The ARFORGEN model ended the tiered readiness levels in the National Guard. Tiered readiness benefitted the enhanced readiness brigades but was a detriment to the other combat brigades.

The longer the conflict persisted, the greater the impact on mobilized reserve forces. On January 19, 2007, Secretary of Defense Gates signed a new policy, "Utilization of the Total Force," that allowed the involuntary mobilization of reservists for a maximum of one year.[3] This policy change affected all the Services, but particularly the Army. Previously, the Services had the ability to involuntarily mobilize reservists for eighteen months, which allowed the Army to train its National Guard Brigade Combat Teams for

---

[2] Alexandra Hemmerly-Brown, "ARFORGEN: Army's Deployment Cycle Aims for Predictability," *Army.Mil*, November 19, 2009, http://www.army.mil/article/30668/ARFORGEN_Army_039_s_deployment_cycle_aims_for_predictability/ (accessed February 29, 2012).

[3] Robert M. Gates, , Memorandum for Secretaries of the Military Departments, et alia, Utilization of the Total Force, January 19, 2007.

six months and deploy them for twelve. Now the Army had to be more judicious with training time. The new policy forced the Army to increase training readiness in the reserve components prior to mobilization, to maximize time for deployment.

The close involvement of congressional leaders with the military, fostered the many legislative changes affecting the armed forces. The Services and the Joint Chiefs of Staff should not be surprised if congressional leaders try to influence what forces will be employed in a contingency, just as combatant commanders will request forces task organized to fulfill specific requirements. Congress will try to influence the Services to provide reserve forces to the combatant commanders as a means of asserting their legislative authority to ensure tax dollars are being spent for the intended purpose. Goldwater-Nichols gave the combatant commanders additional authorities to select which forces they use. The U.S. Constitution did not create the Combatant Commanders or the Joint Chiefs. However, the Constitution did give Congress the authority to govern the militia. The Constitution specifically states:

> The Congress shall have power to…provide for the common defense…[and]…To raise and support Armies…To provide and maintain a Navy…To provide for organizing, arming and disciplining the militia, and for governing such part of them as may be employed in the service of the United States….[4]

For almost two decades prior to the Persian Gulf War, Congress had authorized and appropriated for the Army to train and equip the roundout brigades in the event the nation were to go to war. The Army did not effectively communicate to Congress why they did not seek to use the roundouts for a conventional war. Elected representatives naturally tried to influence the Secretary of Defense and the Army with what forces should be

---

[4] Constitution of the United States, Article I, Section 8.

employed as a way of verifying the taxpayers' investment. The Services have a professional obligation to Congress to demonstrate when necessary that the citizens' money is being wisely spent for the intended purpose.

The only practical way for the Services to prove that they are spending tax dollars prudently, is to demonstate their level of readiness for combat. The measure of an effectively trained strategic reserve, must be proven through continuous testing of the level of readiness. If the reserve component forces are not being employed for combat, they must be tested. Through the systematic evaluation of training readiness, the U.S. Armed Forces can ensure that the reserve components maintain near-peer proficiency with the active components. For the Army, this means an independent command evaluates training so that the there is no appearance that a parent command inflated training readiness reports as was alleged for the roundout brigades recalled during Operation Desert Shield. If active Army forces are not being employed in combat missions, they must also be tested by an independent Army command. Otherwise there is no proof that the American taxpayer is getting the training readiness they are paying for.

The Army must employ its reserve component forces when the demand for forces exceeds what the active component can supply. As demand goes down, so will the need to employ reserve component forces. When not employed, unit training readiness must be effectively evaluated. There is no funding for a systematic program to evaluate training readiness. The National Defense Act of 1916 funded the reserve components for 48 drill periods (one weekend a month) and fifteen days annual training (two weeks a year). That is all the training time available to a reserve unit. The funding to evaluate training outside the 48 drill periods and 15 days, must come from the Services' budgets.

There is tension between the active and reserve components of the Services, especially within the Army, that has been present since the training camps prior to World War I. It is natural that this tension exists because the components compete within a Service for the same resources - whether it be facilities, personnel, equipment, or training dollars. This tension can be divisive and centrifugal in nature moving the active and reserve components away from each other. The reserve components and active components often fight over the same scarce resources. There is an opposing tension that can be cohesive and centripetal in nature as the reserve and active components face the same enemy in the homeland or overseas. The reserve and active components need each other as part of the all-volunteer force. The successful management of these tensions for the all-volunteer force depends on well-defined roles for both the reserve and active components. The reserve components must accept that they cannot maintain the high level of training readiness to be the first deploying combat forces for any worldwide contingency. The active components must accept that they will never match the response time of the reserves and National Guard to domestic emergencies. Ensuring training readiness matches the roles and capabilities of each component while limiting divisive forces between active and reserve components.

Engagement with American Society

Much of the active military has traditions and culture that diverges from the rest of American society.[5] There are no professions in American society that value superior tank gunnery skills or precision bombing. As the military gets smaller, it becomes less

---

[5]David R.Segal and Karin De Angelis, "Changing Conceptions of the Military as a Profession," *American Civil Military Relations*, ed. Suzanne C. Nielsen and Don M. Snider (Baltimore, MD: The John Hopkins University Press, 2009), 206.

representative of American society. This is the fear that the Gates Commission addressed when it predicted that an all-volunteer force would *not* become further detached from society. The citizen-soldiers of the reserve component are an important link for the soldier-citizens of the active component back to American society. This is an important symbiotic relationship. The citizen-soldiers of the total force help to keep the active military force from becoming too divergent, and therefore too isolated, from American society. The citizen-soldiers of the National Guard and Reserves represent their Services in every state and territory of the United States, whereas 70 percent of the active force is based in only 10 states.[6] Citizen-soldiers can effectively lobby Congress without professional reservations except for the one weekend a month and two weeks a year that they are serving in a military capacity. Providing the citizen-soldier believes that the military is one team, the armed forces reap the benefits of representation sown in all fifty states, the three unincorporated organized territories and the District of Columbia. When citizen-soldiers are full members of the military team, they reap the benefits of professional development and better training opportunities afforded by the active force. The U.S Military benefits with an extended team of active and reserve soldiers – a truly total force military, vice one in name only.

---

[6]Mark Thompson, "The Other 1%," *Time*, November 21, 2011, 36.

CHAPTER 4: CONCLUSION

The Total Force evolved through painful lessons in our country's history. The force structure for the active Army was too small for the expeditionary nature of the Spanish-American War. Poor force structure decisions adversely affected the training time and performance of Army National Guard units in World War I. Poor training readiness of National Guard combat units prior to World War II and the Persian Gulf War demonstrated the need to need to quantify and evaluate peacetime training. Because the Services depend more on their reserve components now, than in previous times in U.S. history, our small, all-volunteer force must be closely integrated to ensure the ability of the Total Force to respond quickly to threats to national security.

Recommendations

The following recommendations are offered to improve the Total Force Concept:

1. Accountable public officials must make holistic force structure decisions throughout each Service. We cannot afford excessive force structure. Although reserve component force structure is less than one-third the cost of active component force structure, any excess force structure steals funding from equipping, personnel readiness and training.[7] The naturally competing components of a Service will seldom universally welcome force structure decisions; each component is vying for the same scarce resources. The very political nature of force structure decisions combined with the obligation to wisely spend taxpayer dollars require the secretary of defense or the president make force structure decisions. In 1993, Secretary of Defense Aspin allowed

---

[7] The metrics for measuring the costs of the reserve components vary significantly. Just considering personnel costs, for the reserve components there are 48 drill periods and 15 days of annual training, or 63 total days. Personnel costs for the active component are 365 days.

the Army to make its own force structure decisions. The Army deferred the force structure decisions to an "offsite" committee consisting of members of each component and unofficial military organizations. Consensus became the means to make decisions for the committee. According to the Government Accountability Office, the subsequent restructuring cost ten times the original estimate.[8]

2. Capability must drive missions, irrespective of component. Missions that require limited training during peacetime and have a short deployment requirement are better suited to the reserve component. Missions that require long deployments are better suited to the active component since long deployments test the limits of citizen-soldiers who are away from their civilian jobs. It makes more sense to have active component units fill early deploying combat missions. If we rely on calling up the reserve component for every contingency, we risk testing the limits of the citizen-soldier. Those missions that readily converge with civilian job skills such as pilots, stevedores, and medical personnel more readily translate to early deploying reserve component missions. Despite the reserve components willingness to prove themselves equal to their active component counterparts, good intentions do not overcome limited training time.[9] Missions chosen must not be for duration or desirability but for proven capability.

3. Services must quantify training requirements at the appropriate unit level. The smaller a unit is, the easier it is to define training requirements and the more attractive that unit becomes for a Service to nominate for employment. This means that the Marines will have much less difficulty defining requirements to get a tank company

---

[8] Duncan, 237-238.
[9] Ibid., 221.

ready for combat than the Army will have in defining the training requirements for a heavy brigade. It is much easier for the Air Force to define training gates to track training readiness progression for an aircrew than for an entire squadron. The more objectively and precisely defined that training requirements are, the easier it is to evaluate and maintain combat readiness.

4. Each Service must regularly test readiness. After quanitifying training requirements, the four Services must test readiness. The Army would do well to take a few lessons from the Air Force ability to progressively show training readiness through gates. Each Service must maintain the capability to test readiness and exercise that capability across both its reserve and active components. With shrinking defense budgets, the United States cannot afford to wait for the order to deploy military forces before determining if the forces are ready for combat. The Services use supplemental funding to train and test forces before deploying for combat. No permanent policy exists to test units not deploying for combat. The Services must bear the cost of testing in their base budgets without relying on supplemental funding. Excess force structure in any area must be trimmed to allow each Service to fence force structure needed to test training readiness. To ensure consistent standards of readiness, the force structure dedicated to testing training readiness should evaluate reserve and active forces alike. Only when the same training standards apply equally across a Service or capability can the components complement each other's capabilities.

5. Peacetime missions must support training for combat missions or readiness will decline. The missions for U.S. defense forces have burgeoned since the 1990's. U. S. military forces now participate in disaster relief, humanitarian assistance, patrolling the borders for illegal aliens (Southern Watch), security and advisory assistance (including Partnership for Peace), counter-piracy, and arms control. Although peacekeeping missions generally require the same skills as support forces use in combat such as moving equipment and personnel, these missions seldom require combat forces to utilize the same skills that will be employed during war. Unless peacetime missions support skills required during combat, limited training time is lost to duties other than maintaining combat training readiness. Ultimately, readiness suffers. Peacetime missions must have a lower priority than validation of combat skills.

These five recommendations offer a simple framework to ensure continued improvement to the Total Force Concept. The most important of these recommendations is the need for the Services, especially the Army, to place increased emphasis on training readiness through the systematic testing of reserve component training. As Service budgets get smaller this will become increasingly difficult. The 48 drill periods and 15 days of annual training are insufficient for RC units to both train and be tested. Any additional testing days will have to be funded by the Services. The Services will also have to dedicate force structure to testing, when reductions in force structure threaten core missions. The Services will have to sacrifice force structure and base budget funding to test reserve component training. Testing the reserve component will reinforce the foundation for a solid relationship between the active and reserve forces. Training readiness of the reserve components will ensure integration between the active and reserve forces fostering teamwork which allows for the reserve component citizen-soldiers to lobby legislators on behalf of the Total Force instead of just their component. The integration of the Total Force gained from testing training readiness of the reserve components preserves the structure and skills needed for combat, thus ensuring our

nation is prepared for future conflicts.

BIBLIOGRAPHY

Abrams, Jr., Creighton W. *The Sixteen Division Force: Anatomy of a Decision*. Ft.
    Belvoir: Defense Technical Information Center, 1975.
    http://handle.dtic.mil/100.2/ADB006176 (accessed November 15, 2011).

Bradley, Omar Nelson, and Clay Blair. *A General's Life: An Autobiography*. New York:
    Simon and Schuster, 1983.

Brayton, Abbott A. "American Reserve Policies Since World War II". *Military
    Affairs* 36, no. 4 (December 1972): 139-144.

Buchalter, Alice R. and Seth Allen. *Historical Attempts to Reorganize the Reserve
    Components*. Washington, DC: Library of Congress, 2007.

Carafano, James Jay. *The Army Reserves and the Abrams Doctrine: Unfulfilled Promise,
    Uncertain Future*. Washington, DC: Heritage Foundation, 2005.

Doubler, Michael D. *I Am the Guard A History of the Army National Guard, 1636-2000*.
    Washington, DC: Army National Guard, 2001.

Duncan, Stephen M. *Citizen Warriors: America's National Guard and Reserve Forces &
    the Politics of National Security*. Novato, CA: Presidio, 1997.

Faltinson, Brian. "A Crisis Hits Home." *National Guard*, August 2011, 92-95.

Goldich, Robert L. *The Army's Roundout Concept After the Persian Gulf War*.
    Washington, DC: Congressional Research Service, Library of Congress, 1991.

Government Accountability Office. *National Guard Peacetime Training Did Not
    Adequately Prepare Combat Brigades for Gulf War : Report to the Secretary of the
    Army*. Washington, DC: The Government Printing Office, 1991,
    http://archive.gao.gov/d19t9/144875.pdf (accessed January 23, 2012).

Gross, Charles J. , "A Chronological History of the Air National Guard and its
    Antecedents, 1908-2007," April 2, 2007,
    http://www.ngb.army.mil/features/AF60th/ANG-CHRON_1908_2007.doc
    (accessed October 12, 2011).

Harris, Brian C. "Relevance of Army National Guard Infantry Units in the Force
    Structure and Their Role in Combat," Carlisle Barracks, PA: U.S. Army War College,
    2004. http://handle.dtic.mil/100.2/ADA423614 (accessed October 10, 2011).

Kinnard, Douglas. *The War Managers: American Generals Reflect on Vietnam*. New
    York, NY: Da Capo Press, 1991.

Lacy, James L. "Naval Reserve Forces: The Historical Experience with Involuntary

Recalls," Alexandria, VA: Center for Naval Analyses, 1986.

Lee, Gus C., and Geoffrey Y. Parker. *Ending the Draft: The Story of the All Volunteer Force*. Alexandria, VA: Human Resources Research Organization, 1977.

McQuiston, I. M. "History of the Reserves Since the Second World War," *Military Affairs,* 17, 23-27. no. 1, 1953.

Melnyk, Les'. *Mobilizing for the Storm The Army National Guard in Operations Desert Shield and Desert Storm*. Arlington, VA: National Guard Bureau, Office of Public Affairs, Historical Services Division, 2001. http://purl.access.gpo.gov/GPO/LPS28302 (accessed November 2, 2011).

National Defense Research Institute (U.S.). *Assessing the Structure and Mix of Future Active and Reserve Forces. Final Report to the Secretary of Defense*. Santa Monica, CA: RAND, 1992.

Philbin, Edward J. and James L. Gould, " The Guard and Reserve: In Pursuit of Full Integration," in *The Guard and Reserve in the Total Force.* Edited by Bennie J. Wilson III, Washingto, DC: National Defense University Press, 1985.

Reimer, Dennis J., Roger C. Schultz, and James R. Helmly. The Independent Panel Review of Reserve Component Employment in the Era of Persistent Conflict. Washington, DC: Department of the Army, 2010.

Schwarzkopf, H. Norman, and Peter Petre. *It Doesn't Take a Hero: General H. Norman Schwarzkopf, the Autobiography*. New York: Bantam Books, 1992.

Segal, David R. and Karin De Angelis. "Changing Conceptions of the Military as a Profession," in *American Civil-Military Relations: The Soldier and the State in a New Era,* 194-212. Edited by Suzanne C. Nielsen and Don M. Snider. Baltimore, MD: Johns Hopkins University Press, 2009.

Sorley, Lewis. "Reserve Components: Looking Back to Look Ahead." Joint Force Quarterly 36 (December 2004): 18-23, http://www.dtic.mil/doctrine/jel/jfq_pubs/0536.pdf (accessed May 30, 2012).

Sorley, Lewis. *Thunderbolt: General Creighton Abrams and the Army of His Times.* Bloomington, IN: Indiana University Press, 2008.

United States. *Making Appropriations for the Department of Defense: Conference Report (to Accompany H.R. 5803)*. Washington, DC: Government Printing Office, 1990.

United States. *Merger of the Army Reserve Components. Hearings Before Subcommittee No.2, Eighty-Ninth Congress, First Session*. 1965.

United States. *Subcommittee Hearings on H.R. 8373, to Provide for the Acquisition, Construction, Expansion, Rehabilitation, Conversion, and Joint Utilization of Facilities Necessary for the Administration and Training of Units of the Reserve Components of the Armed Forces of the United States, and for Other Purposes.* Washington, DC: Government Printing Office, 1950.

United States. *Hearing on National Defense Authorization Act for Fiscal Year 2011 and Oversight of Previously Authorized Programs Before the Committee on Armed Services, House of Representatives, One Hundred Eleventh Congress, Second Session Readiness Subcommittee Hearing on Budget Request for Army Reserve, Army National Guard, and Air National Guard Training and Operations, Hearing Held April 27, 2010.* Washington, DC: Government Printing Office, 2010. http://purl.fdlp.gov/GPO/gpo1314 (accessed November 20, 2011).

United States. *Armed Forces Reserve Act of 1952: With Amendments to December 31, 1955. Public Law 476-82d Congress.* Washington, DC: Government Printing Office, 1955.

United States, and William Richard King. *Achieving America's Goals: National Service or the All-Volunteer Armed Force? : Study.* Washington, DC: Government Printing Office, 1977.

United States. *Progress in Ending the Draft and Achieving the All-Volunteer Force.* Washington, DC: Government Printing Office, 1972.

United States. *The Marine Corps Reserve: A History.* Washington, DC: Government Printing Office, 1966.

United States Army Center for Military History, "Chapter 26, The Army and the New Look," in *American Military History,* April 27, 2001, http://www.history.army.mil/books/AMH/AMH-26.htm (accessed May 23, 2012).